IMPROVIS STARTERS

A Collection of 900 Improvisation Situations for the Theater

Philip Bernardi

BETTERWAY BOOKS
Cincinnati, Ohio

Cover design and photographs by Susan Riley
Typography by Kurt H. Fischer

Improvisation Starters: A Collection of 900 Improvisation Situations for the Theater. Copyright 1992 © by Philip Bernardi. Printed and bound in the United States of America. All rights reserved. No part of this book may be reproduced in any form or by any electronic or mechanical means including information storage and retrieval systems without permission in writing from the publisher, except by a reviewer, who may quote brief passages in a review. Published by Betterway Books, an imprint of F&W Publications, Inc., 1507 Dana Avenue, Cincinnati, Ohio, 45207. 1-800-289-0963. First edition.

96 95 94 93 92   5 4 3 2

Library of Congress Cataloging-in-Publication Data

Bernardi, Philip.
    Improvisation starters: a collection of 900 improvisation situations for the theater/Philip Bernardi.
    p. cm.
    ISBN 1-55870-233-4 (pbk.): $8.95
    1. Improvisation (Acting) I. Title
PN2071.I5B47 1992

792'.028 --dc20

91-42586
CIP

To Carol

Acknowledgments

I wish to thank my wife Carol for her love and support during the preparation of this book; my brother Fred for his invaluable advice; my family and close friends for their encouragement; and the administrators, faculty, and drama students of Pascack Hills High School for giving me the opportunity to try out most of the improvisation starters included in this book.

Contents

Introduction

I once asked a class of beginning actors how they planned to prepare for their first scene assignment. They responded by saying that they would take home their scripts, memorize their lines, and rehearse the scenes over and over until things like timing, movement, and facial expressions were perfect. Almost every student figured on working with script in hand for at least the first few rehearsals. When I suggested that they work *without* using scripts during some of their first rehearsals, they seemed baffled. Work *without* the script? What productive purpose could this possibly serve? At this point in their training, they did not understand the value of improvisation.

Few of us get up in the morning and plan exactly what we will say and do throughout the day. Of course, there are times we might privately rehearse something important that we'd like to say. But even in those situations, we must often adjust our speeches according to the verbal or nonverbal response of the person to whom we are speaking.

A very small part of what we do in life is done with a high degree of intensity. In fact, most of us follow a rather unexciting routine for a good part of our day. We get up in the morning, take a shower, get dressed, make coffee, go to work or school; all done on a rigid schedule and without much thought or concentration. However, life is sometimes very intense and exciting, and these moments of life are the ones that are most memorable.

A play is a reflection of life, regardless of what form of theater we're dealing with. However, a good playwright leaves out what is dull and routine and includes only what is intense and exciting. But how many times have we seen a good play ruined by actors who fail to perform with the proper degree of intensity? Most likely, these actors have had very little training in the art of improvisation.

During an improvisation, the actor is forced to react spontaneously to what is happening on stage. All his concentration is directed toward the situation and the other actors in the scene. Since no script has been read, the actor has no preconceived way to play the scene. Nothing that happens in an improvisation is planned very far in advance, so the scene naturally has the same freshness and vigor as a moment of real life. If strong enough conflicts are suggested, the improvisation will maintain a good level of intensity. With enough practice, the actor gradually begins to realize that every performance of a staged play must be performed with the same level of energy as an improvisation.

While most theater teachers realize the value of improvisation as a regular part of their classes, many find it difficult to come up with fresh ideas on a daily basis. The nine hundred improvisation ideas included in this book should provide most theater teachers with enough material to last for more than a year.

1

Using Character Conflicts

Life is filled with conflict. Our everyday dealings with the people
we encounter can result in conflict. We may try to escape conflict,
but sometimes it's unavoidable, especially when the other people
involved have agendas that are completely different from our
own. It's in those situations that we must find a way to resolve our
conflicts so that we can accomplish our objectives.

A strong conflict can provide the foundation for an excellent
improvisation. This chapter contains many suggestions for using
conflicting character objectives to start an improvisation. The ideas
in this chapter are intended for use by two players at a time, but
many may be adjusted to involve three or more.

The instructor should conduct the improvisations in the following way: Ask the players to take the stage or playing area. The
stage or playing area should be bare, except for three or four chairs
that the players may wish to use during the improvisation. Assign
each player a role and read the scene description of the improvisation starter aloud. Immediately after doing this, provide each
player with his or her own objective. This may be done by whisper-
ing it to each player privately, or by writing it on a slip of paper and
handing it to the player. *It is important that the players do not know
each other's objectives in advance.* As soon as they understand their
objectives, signal them to begin.

Before beginning, review the following guidelines with your
players:

1. Keep your objective in mind at all times during the impro-
    visation. Everything you say or do must be directed toward
    accomplishing your objective. If you find that what you're
    doing to accomplish your objective is not working, then try
    something else. However, the *objective itself* should *not* be

changed. Your objective provides the energy and focus necessary to keep the scene moving.

2. After your instructor provides you with your objective, don't ask for any further elaboration. Make up any other details that you feel you require to perform the improvisation, but don't change the objective.

3. Focus only on the other actor(s), *not* the audience. All outward expression should result from an honest reaction to the situation, not from what you think the audience should be seeing. Don't play emotions; just become involved in the situation. Do what you would normally do in that particular circumstance; don't try to be "dramatic." You're not writing a play, you're simply trying to reach your objective.

4. Go along with any new element introduced by your partner. If your partner says that he is married, don't question it. (Unless, of course, you believe that he is lying!)

5. You may use chairs, but pantomime the use of any other objects that may be necessary.

6. Don't respond to the other players by speaking or behaving in a typical fashion. Don't play the "rebellious teenager" or the "pushy salesman." Just behave *normally*!

7. Continue trying to accomplish your objective until the instructor tells you to stop. Remember, if you think you're getting nowhere with one line of action, try another.

After each improvisation, you may wish to discuss the performance with your players and the audience. You may use the following questions to guide your discussion:

1. How closely did the players stick to their objectives? Did any of the players try to change their objectives?

2. What specific strategies did the players use to try to accomplish their objectives? What specific actions did the players choose to carry out those strategies? Did each player use an original or a creative approach?

3. Did the players do anything that seemed phony or contrived? Were any guilty of playing to the audience instead of to the other player?

4. Did any character element seem to be stereotyped?

5. Did any of the players break concentration during the improvisation?

6. Was there too much talk and too little action?

7. Did the players use their imaginations well?

IMPORTANT NOTE: Unless a specific gender is required, the roles described in the following improvisation situations may be played by either males or females. For consistency, most are written from the male point of view; but in almost every case, you may replace "he" with "she," "man" with "woman," "boy" with "girl," "father" with "mother," "husband" with "wife," "son" with "daughter," etc.

TEEN/PARENT CONFLICTS

1 **THE SCENE:** A teenager is discussing with his father his intention to go to a party next week.

Teen's Objective: The party promises to be especially wild because adults will not be present. Get your father's permission to go.

Father's Objective: You're very reluctant to allow your son to go to any unsupervised party since you're concerned about the presence of drugs or alcohol at such parties. Refuse to let him go to the party.

2 **THE SCENE:** A father and his teenage son are sitting in the living room of their house when they hear a car horn blowing outside. The teen tells his father that his date has arrived; the two are going to the movies. The father has yet to meet the date.

Teen's Objective: You want to leave immediately because the film starts in ten minutes. Rush out of the house as soon as you can!

Father's Objective: You have yet to meet the date. Insist upon meeting the date before they leave.

3 **THE SCENE:** A father and his teenage son are sitting in the teen's bedroom. The mother has just left the house.

Teen's Objective: You realize that your parents are splitting up, and you're trying to resolve the feelings of guilt that you're having. You feel somehow responsible for the situation.

Father's Objective: You want to make sure that your son knows that the problems that exist between you and your wife have nothing to do with him.

4 **THE SCENE:** A father is tasting a meat loaf that his son has just prepared for his family.

Teen's Objective: You're very proud of your accomplishment, and you want your family to enjoy the meal.

Father's Objective: This is the worst meat loaf you've ever tasted. Tell your son what you think, but be careful not to hurt his feelings.

5 **THE SCENE:** A teenager walks into his house after spending the day at a shopping mall. He borrowed his father's brand-new sportscar to get there. The teen's father is in the room when he walks in.

Teenager's Objective: You were in an accident. You're perfectly fine, but the car is badly damaged. The accident was totally your fault, but you don't want your parents to know that.

Father's Objective: You love your new sportscar. You're glad that your son has returned with it because you'd like to wash and wax it.

6 **THE SCENE:** A teenager who has been grounded is attempting to sneak out of the house. Just as he is about to leave, his father walks into the room.

Teen's Objective: Convince your father that you have a good reason for leaving.

Father's Objective: Demand to know why your son is trying to leave.

7 **THE SCENE:** A teenage boy's father notices an earring hanging from his son's left ear.

Teen's Objective: You think the earring looks great. Fight for the right to wear it.

Father's Objective: The idea of your son wearing an earring disturbs you. Have him get rid of it.

8 THE SCENE: A teenager holding a report card walks into his living room where his father is sitting in a chair reading the paper.

Teen's Objective: You need to have a parent sign the card. Unfortunately, you failed every subject except art — you got an "A" in that! You plan to be a freelance artist immediately after high school, so you really don't care about any other grades.

Father's Objective: You are anxious to see your son's report card. You believe good grades in all subjects are very important, and you want your son to go to a good college.

9 THE SCENE: A teenager is discussing with his father the possibility of buying a dog.

Teen's Objective: Promise that if you're given permission to buy a dog, you will take very good care of it.

Father's Objective: You don't want a pet in the house. Refuse to give your permission.

10 THE SCENE: A teenager is discussing with his father his intention to join the Army after high school.

Teen's Objective: You would be proud to serve your country. Convince your father that this is a good idea.

Father's Objective: You're concerned that your child will be hurt or killed in a war. Talk him out of it!

11 THE SCENE: A teenager walks into a room where his father is sitting, figuring out the monthly bills.

Teen's Objective: You have in your hand a biology test that you received from your teacher today. You scored 100% on it, and you're very proud of yourself. Share your enthusiasm with your father.

Father's Objective: You're very busy figuring out the monthly bills. You're also very upset because they amount to much more than you can afford this month. Continue to concentrate on your work and avoid any interruptions or distractions.

12 THE SCENE: A father walks into his teenage son's room to speak with him about his son's whereabouts last night.

Teen's Objective: You said you were at your friend's house last night, but you actually were in a bar. You used false identification to get in. Don't admit the truth.

Father's Objective: Your son said he was at his friend's house last night, but you spoke to his friend a few moments ago. He told you that your son was not with him. Find out the truth.

13 THE SCENE: A father is talking to his teenage son about a girl he's been dating.

Father's Objective: You don't like this young girl your son is dating. Forbid him to see her.

Teen's Objective: You know your father doesn't like the girl you're dating, but you don't care. Refuse to break up with her.

14 THE SCENE: A father is having a private talk with his thirteen-year-old son.

Father's Objective: For one reason or another, you haven't yet told your son that he's adopted. You've decided that the time is now, but you know that you have to be very delicate with his feelings.

Son's Objective: You realize that your father has something very serious that he wants to discuss with you. Find out what it is.

15 THE SCENE: A teenage boy is explaining to his father how to operate a new VCR.

Teen's Objective: You're having a difficult time explaining to your father how the VCR works. He just doesn't seem to comprehend your instructions, yet you're determined to get him to understand.

Father's Objective: You're determined to figure out how the VCR works, but you're very confused by all the buttons on the thing.

STUDENT/TEACHER CONFLICTS

16 **THE SCENE:** A teacher and a student are in a high school classroom. The bell has just sounded indicating the end of the class period, when the teacher asks the student to stay and talk for a few minutes.

Teacher's Objective: You've found some drug paraphernalia under the student's desk, and you think it belongs to the student. Offer to help your student find help for his drug problem.

Student's Objective: You've been forced to hold onto drug paraphernalia by another student who has threatened to hurt you unless you comply. Tell your teacher about this, but make him promise not to tell anyone else.

17 **THE SCENE:** A parachuting instructor is about to give a student the signal to make his first jump.

Instructor's Objective: You've had 100% success with dozens of previous parachuting students, and you want to maintain your perfect record.

Student's Objective: You suddenly become very frightened. Refuse to jump out of the plane!

18 **THE SCENE:** An English teacher and his student are in the teacher's office discussing a possible grading error on a test.

Teacher's Objective: You are a proud teacher who will not admit to making a error.

Student's Objective: You're certain that the teacher made a mistake. Demand that he rescore your paper and give you a higher grade.

 THE SCENE: A history teacher and his student are in the teacher's office to discuss a research paper assignment.

Teacher's Objective: You believe that the student is not capable of writing a paper of such high quality. Make him confess that he plagiarized the paper.

Student's Objective: You've worked very hard on your paper. Prove to the teacher that it is entirely your own original work.

20 **THE SCENE:** A gym teacher holding a folded piece of paper runs into one of his students in the hall.

Teacher's Objective: You've found an insulting caricature of yourself on the floor of the locker room. You have reason to believe the student drew the picture. Get a confession out of the teen.

Student's Objective: Convince the teacher that you are innocent of any misdeed.

21 **THE SCENE:** A student walks into his English teacher's office to speak with him about the poetry that he's teaching in class.

Student's Objective: You've been chosen by the other students in your class to speak on their behalf. The class feels that studying poetry is a waste of time. Convince the teacher to eliminate poetry from the class curriculum.

Teacher's Objective: You are aware that your students do not enjoy poetry, but you're sure that they will soon see its value.

22 **THE SCENE:** A senior high school student has been called into the principal's office for an important meeting the day before graduation.

Principal's Objective: You've just met with this student's science teacher who has informed you that the student failed his class. Tell the student that because of the failure, he will not be graduating.

Student's Objective: You realize that you may not be graduating because you failed science. However, you think your science teacher has averaged your grade incorrectly. Explain this to the principal.

23 **THE SCENE:** A student has made an appointment to speak with his history teacher in the teacher's office concerning the student's partner in a group research assignment.

Student's Objective: You have a problem with a student you were assigned to work with — you hate him! Beg the teacher to assign you a different partner.

Teacher's Objective: You believe all students should learn to get along with each other. Refuse to make any changes.

SALESMAN/CUSTOMER CONFLICTS

24 **THE SCENE:** A homeowner answers his front door and finds a door-to-door vacuum cleaner salesman.

Salesman's Objective: You want to sell a vacuum cleaner, so you toss a handful of dirt inside the door of the house. Demonstrate just how powerful your vacuum cleaner is.

Homeowner's Objective: You are not in the mood to deal with any salesman. Get rid of him!

25 **THE SCENE:** A customer wants to talk to a used car salesman about a problem he's been having with a car that he bought from him last week.

Salesman's Objective: Convince the customer that the car was fine when you sold it to him, and that you can't be held responsible for anything that may have gone wrong with the car since then.

Customer's Objective: You are sure that something was wrong with the car when you bought it. Demand a full refund.

26 **THE SCENE:** A furniture salesman is speaking to a customer in the showroom of a furniture store that is about to close in ten minutes. The customer, the only one in the store, wants to buy a sofa.

Salesman's Objective: You need to sell $1,000 worth of merchandise in order to win a bonus trip to Hawaii, but in order to qualify, you must do it today before the store closes. Get the customer to buy a $1,000 sofa.

Customer's Objective: You want to buy a particular sofa that sells for $900. Tell the salesman that you're not interested in any other sofa.

27 **THE SCENE:** A cashier tells a customer that his credit card has been rejected.

Customer's Objective: You can't believe that your credit card has been rejected. You just used it in another store, and there was no problem. Convince the cashier that your credit is perfectly good and that something must be wrong with their system.

Cashier's Objective: You are not permitted to sell an item to a customer whose credit card is not accepted. Insist upon cash from this customer, or there will be no sale.

PEER RELATIONSHIP CONFLICTS

28 THE SCENE: A teenager at a party offers another teenager a beer and a cigarette. Almost everyone at the party is smoking and drinking.

First Teen's Objective: You've never before smoked cigarettes or drunk beer, and you don't want to start now. Turn down all offers.

Second Teen's Objective: You think that smoking and drinking are cool. Persuade the other teen to indulge.

29 THE SCENE: A teenager wants to share with his friend his excitement about a letter that he received from a college that he'd like to attend.

Teen's Objective: You open the letter and discover that it's a rejection. You are very upset about this, but you try to hide your feelings.

Friend's Objective: You never thought that your friend would be accepted to this college, but you didn't have the guts to tell him. Console him when you find out that the letter is a rejection.

30 THE SCENE: Two teenage friends are discussing a new kid who has moved into town.

First Teen's Objective: You think this new kid is terrific, and you'd like to invite him to hang around with you and your friends.

Second Teen's Objective: You think this new kid is a jerk, and you don't want anything to do with him.

31 THE SCENE: A teen meets another teen in the hallway of his school.

First Teen's Objective: You are angry because you heard the other teen was spreading awful rumors about you. Confront him and find out why he's been telling lies about you.

Second Teen's Objective: You are intimidated by this other teen, and you would never do anything to cross him. Do everything you can to stay on his good side.

32 **THE SCENE:** Two teenage friends are looking at the basketball team's cut list that's posted on the door of the school gymnasium.

First Teen's Objective: You've been cut from the team. You're very surprised because you think you're an excellent basketball player, certainly much better than your friend. Try to save face by pretending that you really don't want to be part of the team anyway.

Second Teen's Objective: You made the team, but you don't want to show too much enthusiasm because you see that your friend was cut.

33 **THE SCENE:** A teenager meets his friend at his house. The friend just got a new haircut.

Teen's Objective: You think your friend's haircut looks awful. Tell him what you think, but try not to hurt his feelings.

Friend's Objective: You love your haircut, but you value your friend's opinion. Find out what he thinks.

34 **THE SCENE:** A teen meets another teen outside his history class minutes before class is to begin.

First Teen's Objective: You did not study for a test that's being given in class today. Convince the other teen to let you see his answers during the test.

Second Teen's Objective: You are a model student, and you would never dream of cheating.

35 **THE SCENE:** A teen meets his friend to discuss something very important with him.

Teen's Objective: Last night you saw your friend's girlfriend with another guy, and you feel that he has to know for his own good.

Friend's Objective: You suspect that your friend wants to discuss your girlfriend with you. You think that he is jealous because you have a beautiful girlfriend, and he probably would love to see the two of you break up.

36 **THE SCENE:** Two teens are the only ones left at a party that has just taken place in the first teen's house. It's late, and the second teen is about to leave.

First Teen's Objective: You notice that your wallet is missing. You believe the second teen has it because you think you saw him snooping around your bedroom during the party. Demand that he return the wallet.

Second Teen's Objective: You want to leave quickly because you've taken the first teen's wallet. You took his wallet because you believe he stole *your* wallet at a party you both attended last week.

37 **THE SCENE:** Two high school students are standing outside their principal's office to talk to him about a student whom they have seen dealing drugs. Just as they are about to walk in, the first student changes his mind about seeing the principal.

First Student's Objective: You're afraid of retaliation from the drug dealer, so you don't want to go in.

Second Student's Objective: You need another student to back up your story. Convince the other student to talk.

38 **THE SCENE:** Two teenage friends are enjoying themselves at a party when one of them notices the time. It's almost midnight.

First Teen's Objective: You promised your parents that you'd be home by twelve. Convince your friend to leave with you.

Second Teen's Objective: You're having a great time, and you don't want to leave. Convince your friend to stay a little longer.

39 **THE SCENE:** Two teenage friends are walking to a shopping mall that's two miles away when one teen makes the suggestion that they should start hitchhiking.

First Teen's Objective: Talk your friend into hitchhiking to the mall; you will get there faster.

Second Teen's Objective: You don't want to hitchhike; you think it's dangerous. Convince your friend that it's much safer to walk.

40 THE SCENE: Two teenagers are standing on the edge of a rooftop of a tall building. About four feet separates this building from another building exactly the same height.

First Teen's Objective: Dare the other teen to jump from this rooftop to the rooftop of the next building.

Second Teen's Objective: You are afraid of heights, so you refuse to do it.

41 THE SCENE: A teenage boy stops another teenage boy in the hall of their high school.

First Teen's Objective: You've heard rumors that this guy was out with your girlfriend last night, and you want to find out if those rumors are true.

Second Teen's Objective: You were out with this guy's girl-friend last night, and you'd like to avoid him.

42 THE SCENE: A high school student interrupts his friend who is studying in the school library.

First Student's Objective: You heard some great gossip about a teacher in the school, and you just have to tell your friend what you heard.

Second Student's Objective: You have a big test next period, and you don't have much time left to study. You don't want to be interrupted for even a moment.

43 THE SCENE: One teen meets a rival student in a corridor of his school.

First Teen's Objective: You heard that this guy's father lost his job, and you taunt him unmercifully about it.

Second Teen's Objective: You're feeling awful because your father, through no fault of his own, lost his job. You love your father and would say or do anything to defend him.

44 **THE SCENE:** Two teens have just stolen a final exam from a teacher's desk.

First Teen's Objective: You're feeling guilty about what you did, and you've decided that you want to put it back before it's discovered missing.

Second Teen's Objective: You want to make copies immediately and sell them to other students.

45 **THE SCENE:** Two teenage friends are sitting on a pier fishing. One teenager has had great success; the other hasn't caught a fish all day.

First Teen's Objective: You attribute your success to the bait that you're using. You've noticed that your friend is using something else. Convince him that he's using the wrong bait.

Second Teen's Objective: You think that your luck will change at any moment. You have full confidence in your methods and you don't want to change anything that you're doing.

46 **THE SCENE:** A teenager opens a letter in front of his friend.

First Teen's Objective: The letter you've opened is an invitation to a party. You don't want your friend to see it because you know that he wasn't invited.

Second Teen's Objective: You can tell by the expression on your friend's face that the letter is extremely fascinating. Demand that he show it to you.

EMPLOYER/EMPLOYEE CONFLICTS

47 **THE SCENE:** An usher at a movie theater has been called into the theater manager's office.

Manager's Objective: You heard from another employee that the usher has been letting his friends into the theater for free. Interrogate him.

Usher's Objective: Another employee at this theater hates you because even though you were hired after he was, you make more money than he does. You think that he has been spreading lies about you. Defend yourself.

48 **THE SCENE:** The owner of a convenience store is talking to his manager about the performance of a recently hired employee.

Owner's Objective: You are not satisfied with the performance of an employee who was hired by your manager. Have him fire this incompetent person.

Manager's Objective: You are aware of the poor performance of an employee whom you recently hired, but try to defend him because he is a good friend of yours.

49 **THE SCENE:** A cashier at a supermarket walks into the supermarket manager's office to ask about a raise.

Cashier's Objective: You've been working at this supermarket for a year now, and you think it's about time you were given a raise. Demand a one dollar increase in your hourly wage.

Manager's Objective: You know that the cashier is one of your best employees, but you have been instructed by your superiors to freeze all wages for the time being.

50 **THE SCENE:** The editor-in-chief of a newspaper has just assigned a new reporter to do a story on a new surgical procedure that's been developed.

Editor's Objective: Inform the reporter that he will need to observe surgeons performing an operation.

Reporter's Objective: You are anxious to make a good impression on your boss, and you are willing to accept any assignment — except one that has to do with blood; you faint at the sight of it.

51 THE SCENE: A manager of a department store has ordered one of his salesmen to sweep the floors because the custodian called in sick.

Manager's Objective: Even though sweeping isn't part of the salesman's responsibilities, you're in a bind. Convince him to do you this one favor.

Salesman's Objective: You weren't hired to sweep floors. Refuse to cooperate with this request.

52 THE SCENE: An executive has just given his secretary a huge pile of file folders to organize and file before the end of work at five o'clock today. It's now 4:30.

Executive's Objective: You think your secretary is perfectly capable of doing the job in half an hour. Insist that the job be completed by five.

Secretary's Objective: You think your boss is crazy. You can't possibly finish the job in half an hour. Promise to finish the job by noon tomorrow.

53 THE SCENE: A factory worker asks his boss about getting some time off. The worker has already used all his allotted personal days.

Worker's Objective: You need to take a few days off to visit your sick mother who is resting in a hospital on the other side of the country. Beg for a few additional personal days.

Boss' Objective: You suspect that your employee is lying about why he needs time off. Refuse to grant him any additional personal leave.

54 **THE SCENE:** The manager of a bank is in the process of firing one of his tellers.

Teller's Objective: Yesterday you overheard the bank manager promise his nephew that he'd find a job for him; you think that he's giving your job to him. Accuse your boss of nepotism.

Bank Manager's Objective: You insist that you're firing this teller because of his poor work performance.

CO-WORKER CONFLICTS

55 **THE SCENE:** A singer and his piano accompanist are discussing the possibility of including some new songs in their act.

Singer's Objective: You're sick of doing the same old songs. Convince your partner to include some contemporary songs in your act.

Accompanist's Objective: Your philosophy is, "If it isn't broken, don't fix it." Convince your partner to leave the act alone.

56 **THE SCENE:** A supermarket cashier notices another cashier stealing from a cash register.

First Cashier's Objective: You like your fellow worker, and you'd hate to see him get in trouble. Convince him to put the money back.

Second Cashier's Objective: Deny that you've taken any money from the cash register.

57 **THE SCENE:** A construction worker notices that another worker is not using his hammer properly.

First Construction Worker's Objective: Your partner is hammering nails incorrectly. Show him the proper way to do it.

Second Construction Worker's Objective: You're doing just fine. Continue to hammer nails your way.

58 **THE SCENE:** Two English professors are discussing the question of who really wrote Shakespeare's plays.

First Professor's Objective: You believe all theories about someone else writing Shakespeare's plays are totally ridiculous and unfounded.

Second Professor's Objective: You suggest that the Earl of Oxford actually wrote Shakespeare's plays, based on your belief that only a noble lord could have written the plays.

59 **THE SCENE:** Two cooks in a restaurant's kitchen are preparing a beef stew for the day's special.

First Cook's Objective: Oregano is an important part of your beef stew recipe. Insist that it be included.

Second Cook's Objective: You know how much your fellow cook loves to use oregano, but you don't think that it belongs in the beef stew.

60 **THE SCENE:** Two cleaning service workers are cleaning the living room of a house when one of the workers starts sweeping dust underneath a rug.

First Worker's Objective: You don't see anything wrong with sweeping dust under a rug; you do it all the time! Continue to do it.

Second Worker's Objective: You can't believe what you're seeing! Insist that your fellow worker sweep the dust into a dust pan and dispose of it properly.

61 **THE SCENE:** Two painters are standing at the foot of a twenty-foot ladder leaning against a house.

First Painter's Objective: You've just come down from the ladder after painting a section of the upper part of the house. It's time for you to take a break. Ask your co-worker to finish the job.

Second Painter's Objective: You are deathly afraid of heights, but you're reluctant to admit this. Avoid going up that ladder.

62 **THE SCENE:** A police chief in charge of homicide investigations is in his office with one of his homicide detectives. They're discussing a case that the detective has been working on for months.

Chief's Objective: The detective has already spent too much time on this case and hasn't solved it yet. You're closing the books on this case.

Detective's Objective: You know that you've devoted more time than usual to this case, but you're certain that you can wrap it up successfully within a week. You need a little more time.

63 **THE SCENE:** Two construction workers are digging the foundation of a house when one of them discovers what appears to be a treasure chest.

First Construction Worker's Objective: You think that you may have stumbled upon something very valuable. You'd like to open it right away.

Second Construction Worker's Objective: Try to convince your fellow worker that what he's found is worthless. (You intend to come back when the other worker isn't there and take the chest.)

64 **THE SCENE:** An older accountant is discussing the role of computers in accounting with a younger accountant.

Older Accountant's Objective: You don't believe in computers. An electric adding machine is as sophisticated as you get. Convince the younger accountant that you don't want or need a computer.

Younger Accountant's Objective: You can't believe that the older accountant doesn't use a computer. Convince him that he could do his work much more efficiently and quickly if he used a computer spreadsheet program.

65 **THE SCENE:** After examining the plans for a set of kitchen cabinets that they've just finished building, two carpenters discover that they've used the wrong kind of hinges and knobs on the cabinets.

First Carpenter's Objective: You want to replace all the hinges and knobs, even though you will lose time and money by doing it.

Second Carpenter's Objective: You don't think the homeowners will notice the mistake. You want to leave the wrong hinges and knobs on the cabinets.

66 **THE SCENE:** Two custodians are cleaning out an office when they discover an envelope stuffed with dozens of fifty dollar bills in a wastebasket. It's late at night; no one else is around.

First Custodian's Objective: You want to split the money with your partner and not tell anyone else about your discovery.

Second Custodian's Objective: You want to do the right thing and report your find to your boss.

LOVE RELATIONSHIP CONFLICTS

> **IMPORTANT NOTE:** The roles of the male and female may be reversed in each of the following Love Relationship Conflict situations.

67 **THE SCENE:** A boy is talking to his girlfriend about a phone call that he received from his ex-girlfriend, who called to say that she'd like to maintain a friendship with him.

Boy's Objective: You think it was very nice of your ex-girlfriend to call and say that she wants to be friends. Convince your present girlfriend that she should not feel threatened by your ex-girlfriend.

Girl's Objective: You don't believe for one second that your boyfriend's ex-girlfriend only wants to be friends. You're sure that she wants him back. Make it clear that you want her out of his life.

68 **THE SCENE:** A boy and his girlfriend are trying to decide what movie to go see.

Girl's Objective: You've seen many depressing films with sad endings lately, and you don't want to see another one.

Boy's Objective: You'd like to see a heavily emotional film — the kind that makes you cry at the end.

69 **THE SCENE:** A girl has just prepared a roast beef dinner for her new boyfriend.

Boy's Objective: The roast beef looks like it's been burnt to a crisp. You fear that if you eat it, you will become ill. However, you don't want to hurt your girlfriend's feelings. Force yourself to eat it.

Girl's Objective: You're very proud of the meal that you've prepared, and you'd like to see your boyfriend help himself to seconds.

70 THE SCENE: A boy and his girlfriend are in a restaurant about to order dinner.

Boy's Objective: You are very hungry, so order a huge meal.

Girl's Objective: You've noticed that your boyfriend has gained quite a few pounds in the last few weeks. Persuade him to order something light.

71 THE SCENE: A girl and her boyfriend are sitting in her apartment discussing one of her ex-boyfriends.

Girl's Objective: Convince your present boyfriend that your relationship with your ex-boyfriend is over.

Boy's Objective: Find out if your girlfriend is seeing her ex-boyfriend when you're not around.

72 THE SCENE: A boy and his girlfriend are discussing the future of their relationship.

Boy's Objective: You're very upset because you fear that your girlfriend wants to break up with you. Convince her to give the relationship more time.

Girl's Objective: You realize that you no longer love your boyfriend. However, you still have some feelings for him, and you don't want to hurt him. As gently as possible, break up with him.

73 THE SCENE: A girl is discussing with her ex-boyfriend the possibility of getting back together with him.

Boy's Objective: Your ex-girlfriend hurt you very badly. Convince her that there is no way that you would ever get back together with her.

Girl's Objective: You realize that you treated your ex-boyfriend very poorly. You also realize that he was the greatest guy you've ever dated. Beg him for another chance.

THE SCENE: A girl is about to kiss a boy goodnight on their first date.

Girl's Objective: You're nervous, but you'd like to give your date a kiss.

Boy's Objective: You had a very good time tonight. You like this girl, but you don't want her to kiss you because she has bad breath. Avoid the kiss, but try not to hurt her feelings.

 THE SCENE: A girl is informing her boyfriend that her father doesn't want her to see him ever again.

Girl's Objective: You're afraid of what your father might do to you and your boyfriend if he ever finds the two of you together. Convince your boyfriend that it's best to end the relationship.

Boy's Objective: You don't want to break up with your girlfriend. Convince her to run away with you and never return!

76 **THE SCENE:** A woman meets a man at a party.

Woman's Objective: You think this man is very attractive, and you'd like to get his phone number.

Man's Objective: You're not attracted to this woman at all, but you don't want to hurt her feelings.

77 **THE SCENE:** A teenage boy sits beside a teenage girl at a party.

Boy's Objective: You'd love to dance with this girl, but you're not so confident about your dancing abilities.

Girl's Objective: You'd like to dance with this guy. Get him up on the dance floor.

78 **THE SCENE:** A young man and his girlfriend are sitting in a car discussing the idea of marriage. The two have been involved in a serious relationship with each other for the past three years.

Man's Objective: Persuade your girlfriend to marry you.

Woman's Objective: Convince your boyfriend that it would be best to wait another year before getting engaged. You feel that you're still too young for marriage.

79 **THE SCENE:** A man has just finished painting a room in his house when his wife enters.

Wife's Objective: Your husband painted the room the wrong color. You wanted it painted blue, not beige. Have him paint it over.

Husband's Objective: It's taken you hours to paint this room, and you don't want to paint it again. Convince your wife that beige is a great color for this room.

80 **THE SCENE:** A woman is awake when her husband comes home at three o'clock in the morning.

Husband's Objective: You've been out drinking with your friends, and you've had a few too many. You know your wife disapproves of excessive drinking. Try to hide your drunkenness.

Wife's Objective: You know that your husband has been out with his friends. You hate it when he comes home drunk! Make him sleep on the couch tonight.

81 **THE SCENE:** A husband and wife are in a car on their way to the husband's parents' house for dinner.

Husband's Objective: You know that your wife doesn't enjoy visiting your parents because your mother is overly critical of her. Beg your wife not to say or do anything to start an argument with your mother.

Wife's Objective: You can't stand visiting your in-laws because your mother-in-law loves to criticize everything you do and say. If she starts in on you, you will let her have it!

82 **THE SCENE:** A young married couple are having dinner at home when the wife brings up the subject of planning their first child.

Husband's Objective: Convince your wife to wait a few years before having children, so that you can spend some time alone with each other.

Wife's Objective: You want to have children now, since it's best to have them while you are still young.

83 **THE SCENE:** A husband and wife are making a list of whom to invite to a party that they're hosting next week.

Husband's Objective: You want to invite Uncle Joe. You think that he's the funniest guy you've ever met. Make sure he gets an invitation.

Wife's Objective: The only person that you definitely don't want to invite to this party is Uncle Joe. You think he's an obnoxious loudmouth.

84 **THE SCENE:** A woman is watching her husband trying to repair broken pipes underneath the sink.

Wife's Objective: Your husband is making things worse. Convince him to give up and call a plumber.

Husband's Objective: You're sure that you can fix these pipes. Convince your wife that you will have the problem solved shortly.

85 **THE SCENE:** A man is sitting in the living room of his house when his wife walks in with a new hair style.

Wife's Objective: The hair stylist made a mess of your hair, and you are very upset. Other women in the beauty salon told you that it looks great, but you don't believe them. Get your husband's honest opinion.

Husband's Objective: Your wife's hair looks awful, but you don't want to hurt her feelings.

86 **THE SCENE:** A husband and wife are preparing to leave a hotel room on the last day of their vacation. Check-out time is noon, and it's now about eleven-thirty.

Husband's Objective: You're packed and ready to go, but your wife is still packing. Encourage her to hurry because you don't want to be charged for another day.

Wife's Objective: You haven't nearly finished packing yet, even though check-out time is in a half hour. You're sure that you won't be charged for another day if you're a little bit late checking out.

87 **THE SCENE:** A woman is having a serious talk with her husband.

Wife's Objective: You're convinced that your husband is carrying on with another woman. Inform him that you want a divorce.

Husband's Objective: Convince your wife that you're a faithful husband who has never once cheated on her.

DOCTOR/PATIENT CONFLICTS

88 THE SCENE: A doctor is discussing the results of a physical examination with a patient.

Doctor's Objective: Convince your patient that he's in perfect health.

Patient's Objective: You're convinced that you have some type of fatal disease, and you think your doctor is hiding something from you. Demand to know the truth!

89 THE SCENE: A doctor is discussing the results of a physical examination with a patient who happens to be a heavy smoker.

Doctor's Objective: Your patient has a very serious heart condition, and if he doesn't stop smoking, he won't live much longer. You're especially upset with him because you warned him to stop smoking over a year ago. Convince him that he must stop.

Patient's Objective: Promise your doctor that you will stop smoking from this moment on.

90 THE SCENE: A psychiatrist is in his office talking to a new patient.

Psychiatrist's Objective: Last week you pulled a practical joke on a fellow psychiatrist by having a friend pose as a patient who was convinced that he was a carrot. Ever since, you've been waiting for him to retaliate.

Patient's Objective: You've been having dreams about water spurting out of your head, and you're convinced that you were a garden hose in a previous life. Tell the psychiatrist about your dreams and your theory.

91 THE SCENE: A new doctor is about to examine his first patient.

Doctor's Objective: You are very nervous, and you want to conduct a very professional and thorough examination.

Patient's Objective: This doctor is the only doctor in the area who is affiliated with your medical plan, so you have no choice but to see him. However, you are very nervous because he is a new doctor. Make sure he knows what he's doing.

92 THE SCENE: A doctor is in his office talking to a patient.

Doctor's Objective: Be very sensitive with this patient because you must tell him that he may have a serious heart condition. However, you need to see his test results before you know for sure.

Patient's Objective: You feel great, and you refuse to believe that anything is wrong with you.

93 THE SCENE: A doctor wants to inject a patient, who has just injured his back, with a strong pain killer. The patient is in extreme pain.

Doctor's Objective: Your patient will suffer unbearably without the pain killer. Insist upon giving him this injection.

Patient's Objective: You don't believe in using drugs; you won't even take an aspirin. Refuse to take any medication for your pain.

PLAYER/COACH CONFLICTS

94 **THE SCENE:** A football player is on the sidelines trying to get his coach's attention. Their team is losing by a touchdown, and there's only one minute left on the game clock.

Player's Objective: You think that you can score the winning touchdown. Convince the coach to put you in the game.

Coach's Objective: Your game plan does not include this player. Have him sit down and stop bothering you.

95 **THE SCENE:** During his team's last time out, a basketball coach is talking to a player whom he's about to send into the game. Their team is losing by one point, and only five seconds remain on the game clock. This player is the last eligible player; everyone else has fouled out.

Player's Objective: You can't wait to get into the game and score the winning basket. Convince the coach to let you take the final shot.

Coach's Objective: You're only putting this player in the game because he's the last eligible player. Insist that this player pass the ball to someone else if it should come to him.

96 **THE SCENE:** An angry baseball coach wants to talk to a player who hit a game-winning home run in the last inning of a game that was just played.

Coach's Objective: You are angry with this player because he ignored your signal to bunt. Tell him that if he ever again ignores your signals, he will be benched for the rest of the season.

Player's Objective: You don't know why the coach is so angry. After all, your home run won the game.

97 **THE SCENE:** An ice skater and his coach are discussing the skater's routine before performing it in a competition.

Skater's Objective: You want to include a very difficult triple axel jump in your routine.

Coach's Objective: You know that the skater wants to include a very difficult triple axel in his routine, but don't let him do it.

RESTAURANT CONFLICTS

98 **THE SCENE:** A restaurant customer is complaining to his waiter about a hamburger that he ordered.

Customer's Objective: You ordered a hamburger cooked rare, and you think it's overcooked. Demand another hamburger.

Waiter's Objective: You believe that the customer's hamburger is cooked just right.

99 **THE SCENE:** A customer is ordering a meal from a waiter in a restaurant.

Customer's Objective: You want to know how different foods are cooked, and you have lots of questions about the way several foods on the menu are prepared.

Waiter's Objective: You're in a great hurry. Take the order and move to your next customer as soon as possible.

100 **THE SCENE:** A waiter is serving a meal to a customer who placed his order half an hour ago.

Waiter's Objective: A sudden rush of customers caused a backup in the kitchen. Apologize for the long wait and explain the situation.

Customer's Objective: You're particularly angry because someone sitting at the next table ordered a meal after you did, but he was served before you. Demand an explanation.

101 **THE SCENE:** A customer at a restaurant is questioning his waiter about a side order of onion rings that appeared on his bill.

Customer's Objective: You never ordered a side order of onion rings, but you're being charged for it. Have the waiter make a correction on the bill.

Waiter's Objective: You can't prove it because the table has already been cleared, but you are sure that the customer did order the onion rings and that you did serve them to him. As diplomatically as possible, convince him that he did indeed order the onion rings.

102 THE SCENE: A customer in a non-smoking section of a restaurant is complaining to his waiter about smoke from the restaurant's smoking section that is drifting over to his table.

Customer's Objective: The smoke is bothering you. No other tables are available in the non-smoking section, so you'd like the waiter to tell the smokers in the smoking section to put out their cigarettes.

Waiter's Objective: Politely tell the customer that there is nothing you can do about the smoke that is drifting toward his table.

103 THE SCENE: A waiter is speaking to a customer about a chicken dinner that was just served to him.

Waiter's Objective: The cook just told you that the chicken he served was cooked improperly. If the customer eats it, he may become ill. Offer to replace the customer's meal, but don't let him know the reason why.

Customer's Objective: This meal looks great! You haven't taken a bite out of it yet, but it looks like it's cooked perfectly.

POLICE CONFLICTS

104 THE SCENE: A police officer has just pulled over a driver for speeding.

Officer's Objective: The car you've pulled over was doing 40 miles per hour in a 25 mile per hour zone. Give the driver a speeding ticket.

Driver's Objective: Talk the officer out of giving you a speeding ticket.

105 THE SCENE: A police officer is telling a man that his son has been arrested for shoplifting and is in police custody downtown.

Man's Objective: You can't believe that your son would ever steal anything. You're sure there must be some mistake. Find out exactly what happened.

Officer's Objective: You were the arresting officer. There is no mistake; the boy was shoplifting.

106 THE SCENE: A police officer enters a house after hearing its burglar alarm go off. A teenager is standing there when the officer walks in.

Officer's Objective: Find out what the teenager is doing in the house.

Teen's Objective: Convince the police officer that you live in this house, and that the alarm went off accidentally. You have no identification on you.

107 THE SCENE: A police officer sees an adult trying to break into a locked car.

Officer's Objective: Find out what the adult is doing.

Adult's Objective: Convince the police officer that the car belongs to you, and that you accidentally locked your keys in the car. You have no identification on you.

108 THE SCENE: A police detective is interrogating a robbery suspect for information about the prisoner's partner who escaped capture.

Prisoner's Objective: You're afraid of what your partner in crime will do to you if he finds out that you identified him. Refuse to cooperate with the police.

Detective's Objective: Convince the prisoner that things will go a lot easier on him if he cooperates.

109 THE SCENE: A police officer is standing before a house where a ten-year-old boy is being held hostage by a crazed gunman. One of the boy's parents arrives on the scene.

Officer's Objective: Don't let the boy's parent go into the house!

Parent's Objective: Get past the police officer and go into the house to save your son.

110 THE SCENE: A police officer is trying to question a witness about an auto accident that just occurred. The witness only speaks Spanish, and the officer doesn't understand a word he's saying.

Officer's Objective: Try to figure out a way to get as many details about the accident as possible from the witness.

Witness' Objective: Try somehow to explain to the officer what you saw.

111 THE SCENE: A police officer is talking to a man who is threatening to jump off a twenty-story building.

Officer's Objective: Talk the man out of going through with it.

Man's Objective: You actually don't plan to jump, you just want to attract a huge crowd.

112 THE SCENE: A police sergeant has ordered an officer to go inside a burning building to look for any people who might be trapped.

Officer's Objective: You think this is a job for the Fire Department. Convince the sergeant to let the firefighters handle this.

Sergeant's Objective: You don't think the Fire Department will arrive in time. Demand that the officer take immediate action.

113 THE SCENE: A police officer is in a confessional talking to a priest about a suspected murderer he just saw leave the same confessional.

Officer's Objective: You want to know if the man confessed to a murder. Insist that the priest tell you what the man said.

Priest's Objective: You've taken a sacred vow never to discuss any individual's confession with any other person. Refuse to tell the officer anything about the man's confession.

114 THE SCENE: A person stops a police officer on the street to report a sighting of a UFO.

Person's Objective: Convince the officer that you've just seen a UFO.

Officer's Objective: You're convinced that this person is crazy.

BROTHER/SISTER CONFLICTS

> **IMPORTANT NOTE:** The roles of brother and sister may be reversed in each of the following Brother/Sister Conflict situations.

115 **THE SCENE:** A teenage brother and sister are arguing over the use of the family car.

Brother's Objective: You have a date later, so you need the car tonight.

Sister's Objective: You promised your friends that you'd take them all to the movies tonight. You must have use of the car tonight!

116 **THE SCENE:** A girl sees her brother break an expensive lamp.

Brother's Objective: Convince your sister not to tell your parents what has happened.

Sister's Objective: If your brother does your chores for the next two weeks, you will promise not to tell your parents that your brother broke the lamp.

117 **THE SCENE:** A fifteen-year-old boy walks into his older sister's room to speak with her about two eighteen-year-old girls who are both interested in him.

Brother's Objective: You don't know what to do. You like both of these girls, and you're having a difficult time trying to decide which one to date. Seek your sister's advice.

Sister's Objective: You think both of these girls are too old for your brother. Advise him to date someone his own age.

118 THE SCENE: A boy and his sister are trying to decide who gets the larger of two bedrooms in a new house they just moved into.

Boy's Objective: You, of course, want the larger bedroom.

Girl's Objective: You, of course, want the larger bedroom.

119 THE SCENE: A teenage girl is doing her homework at the kitchen table when her brother walks in to ask a favor.

Brother's Objective: You need to borrow ten dollars so that you can go to the movies with your friends.

Sister's Objective: You're angry with your brother because last night he left the house immediately after dinner, and you got stuck doing the dishes alone.

120 THE SCENE: A teenage girl notices that her brother is wearing one of her earrings.

Sister's Objective: You can't believe that your brother is wearing your earring. Insist that he give it back.

Brother's Objective: You think your sister's earring looks great on you. Offer her some money for it.

121 THE SCENE: A brother and sister have pooled their money and are trying to decide what to buy their father on Father's Day.

Brother's Objective: You think that your father would love some gardening tools.

Sister's Objective: You think that your father would love some power tools.

122 THE SCENE: A girl is watching the only television in her house when her brother walks in.

Sister's Objective: You are watching a movie that will be on for the next two hours. You've been looking forward to seeing this movie for the last few weeks.

Brother's Objective: You want to watch a video tape that you just picked up at the local video store. Your friends will be over in a few minutes to watch it with you.

123 THE SCENE: A teenage boy is doing his math homework when his sister walks into the room.

Brother's Objective: Your math homework is very difficult, but you're too proud to ask for help from your sister, who is a math whiz.

Sister's Objective: You know that your brother isn't a very good math student, and you'd hate to see him fail the subject. Insist on helping him.

124 THE SCENE: A girl is driving her brother home from college when she suddenly realizes she is lost.

Sister's Objective: You insist that you will soon recognize something, so there's no need to stop for directions.

Brother's Objective: You think that the only way you'll find your way home is to stop and ask directions.

OTHER INTERPERSONAL CONFLICTS

125 THE SCENE: Two people run into each other on the street.

First Person's Objective: You can't believe it, but it's someone you haven't seen in ten years! Find out what he's been doing all these years.

Second Person's Objective: This person says he knows you, but you don't recognize him. Fake it until you recognize this person.

126 THE SCENE: A man wearing no jacket is trying to get into a restaurant that requires jackets. He's talking to the restaurateur.

Man's Objective: You have friends inside that you must meet. Persuade the restaurateur to let you in.

Restaurateur's Objective: You don't make exceptions for anyone. Don't let this man inside.

127 THE SCENE: A ticket scalper in the parking lot of a concert hall approaches a prospective customer and tries to sell him a $20 ticket for $100.

Ticket Scalper's Objective: You want to get rid of this ticket as soon as possible, but you don't want to sell it for less than $100.

Customer's Objective: You want to buy the ticket, but not for $100. Persuade the ticket scalper to lower his price.

128 THE SCENE: Two people are standing at the end of a line to go into a movie theater. An usher has just counted the number of people on line and has informed the first person that the last ticket available will go to him.

First Person's Objective: You're thrilled because you've been waiting to see this movie for weeks.

Second Person's Objective: You want to see this movie badly. Convince the person standing in front of you to trade places.

129 THE SCENE: A man on the street stops a passerby and asks him if he wants to buy a watch.

Watch Seller's Objective: You claim that these watches were not stolen, and that you're perfectly within your rights to sell them. Persuade this man to buy one.

Passerby's Objective: You're an undercover police officer. Wait for the right moment to arrest this man whom you suspect of selling stolen property.

130 THE SCENE: Two patients are sitting in a dentist's waiting room. The dentist's receptionist has mistakenly scheduled both patients for the same appointment time.

First Patient's Objective: You want to put off seeing the dentist for as long as possible. Insist that the other patient go first.

Second Patient's Objective: You want to put off seeing the dentist for as long as possible. Insist that the other patient go first.

131 THE SCENE: A newspaper reporter needing information for an article he's writing has stopped a person on the street to ask if he would mind being interviewed.

Reporter's Objective: You're writing an article on capital punishment, and you need to get the man on the street's opinion on the subject. The last five people you stopped refused to cooperate. Persuade this person to sit for a brief interview.

Person on the Street's Objective: You are in a rush to get where you're going; you don't have time to be interviewed.

132 THE SCENE: A person walking along the street notices someone staring into space.

First Person's Objective: This strange person has aroused your curiosity. Find out what he's doing.

Second Person's Objective: You're staring into space as a gag. You know that people will be curious and ask you what you're doing.

133 **THE SCENE:** Two people simultaneously reach for a twenty dollar bill lying on the sidewalk.

First Person's Objective: Insist that you saw the bill first and that it belongs to you.

Second Person's Objective: Insist that you saw the bill first and that it belongs to you.

134 **THE SCENE:** A man is walking along the street when it suddenly begins to pour. He doesn't have an umbrella, so he stops a stranger and asks if he can share his umbrella with him.

First Person's Objective: Looking around, you see no shelter from the rain. You're wearing a new silk suit, and if it gets too wet, it will be ruined. Beg the stranger to let you under his umbrella.

Second Person's Objective: You feel uncomfortable standing so close to a stranger, but out of mercy, you let him under your umbrella.

135 **THE SCENE:** A man is questioning a mail carrier about today's delivery.

Man's Objective: You've been expecting an important letter, and you're sure that it would arrive today. Insist that the mail carrier look through his bag for any letter that he may have misplaced.

Mail Carrier's Objective: You're sure that you've given this man every piece of his mail. Convince him that there is nothing else for him in your bag.

136 **THE SCENE:** A man is talking to his next door neighbor about a mess he found on his front lawn.

Man's Objective: You've found empty beer cans strewn all over your front lawn. Your neighbor had a party last night and you think that he threw them there. Insist that your neighbor clean up the mess.

Neighbor's Objective: You claim that you are not responsible for this man's mess. Refuse to cooperate with him.

137 THE SCENE: A teenager with a radio that's blaring loud rock music is sitting on a seat in a bus across the aisle from an adult.

Teen's Objective: You think that you have a right to play your radio as loud as you like. Refuse to turn it down.

Adult's Objective: The loudness of the music is greatly bothering you. Threaten to take his radio and throw it out the window if he doesn't turn it down.

138 THE SCENE: A senior citizen has just offered a teenager some money for helping him carry his groceries to his car.

Teen's Objective: You don't mind doing a good deed for nothing. Refuse to accept any money.

Senior Citizen's Objective: You find it refreshing that a young person is willing to help out a senior citizen. Insist that he take a few dollars for his efforts.

139 THE SCENE: A nightclub doorman asks a customer to produce identification to prove that he is twenty-one years old.

Customer's Objective: You produce a driver's license that says you're twenty-three. Convince the doorman that the license is real.

Doorman's Objective: You don't believe this person is twenty-one years old. Don't let him in.

140 THE SCENE: On its first day open, a movie theater is running a promotion to give free tickets to the first fifty people who arrive. A moviegoer steps up to the box office and is told that he is the fifty-first person to arrive. If he wants to see the movie, he'll have to pay for a ticket.

Box Office Attendant's Objective: You'd like to let this person in for free, but that wouldn't be fair. Refuse to give him a free ticket.

Moviegoer's Objective: You think that the box office attendant miscounted. Insist that he give you a free ticket.

141 THE SCENE: A representative from the IRS is auditing a man suspected of cheating on his income taxes.

Auditor's Objective: You intend to find out whether or not this person actually cheated on his income taxes. Insist that he produce receipts and other records to prove that he did not.

Man's Objective: You insist that you did not cheat on your taxes. Unfortunately, you don't keep very good records, so it's difficult to prove that you're honest.

142 THE SCENE: A man with a severe case of laryngitis stops someone on the street and tries to communicate with him.

First Person's Objective: You have lost your voice completely; you can't even whisper. You do, however, need to get directions. Figure out a way to communicate with the person you've stopped.

Second Person's Objective: You'd like to help this man. Try to figure out what he wants.

143 THE SCENE: A man hears someone screaming from a building across the street. He stops a passerby and asks if he will help him find out what's going on.

First Person's Objective: You think that someone might be in a great deal of trouble. You fear that if you call the police, they may not be able to show up in time to help whoever is in trouble. Get this person to help you investigate.

Second Person's Objective: You don't want to get involved.

144 THE SCENE: A homeowner calls a plumber because some of his basement pipes are leaking, and his cellar is filling up with water. When the plumber arrives, he insists on twenty dollars cash in advance before he does anything.

Homeowner's Objective: You have no cash on you. You offer him a check or credit card, but he will only accept cash. Find a way to get him to fix your pipes.

Plumber's Objective: You make no exceptions regarding your cash policy. Refuse to help the man unless he produces the cash.

145 **THE SCENE:** A man walks into a German delicatessen to buy food for some unexpected guests who have showed up at his house. The owner is standing behind the counter.

Customer's Objective: It's late at night, and this is the only food store in the neighborhood that's open. Order some cold cuts.

Owner's Objective: All you know how to say in English is, "I don't speak English." Try to communicate with this customer by using gestures and other nonverbal expressions.

146 **THE SCENE:** A paper boy is having trouble getting one of his customers to pay for the papers that he delivered last week.

Paper Boy's Objective: You delivered your papers to this customer and you expect to get paid.

Customer's Objective: You claim that you found your paper in your bushes all week. Once, you even found it on the roof! Refuse to pay the boy.

147 **THE SCENE:** An actor is doing a solo improvisation before the rest of his acting class when the acting teacher stops the improvisation.

Teacher's Objective: You stopped the improvisation because the actor lost track of his objective. Remind him of his objective and have him start over.

Actor's Objective: You lost track of your objective. Start the improvisation over, this time sticking to your objective.

148 **THE SCENE:** A man goes to a barber shop to have his hair trimmed.

Man's Objective: You like your hair style the way it is. All you want is a simple trim.

Barber's Objective: You think this customer would look great with a completely new hair style. Persuade him to try something new.

149 THE SCENE: A prospective home buyer is trying to settle on the price of a house from the seller. The asking price of the home is $190,000.

Buyer's Objective: Talk the seller down to $170,000.

Seller's Objective: Don't take anything less than $180,000 for the house.

150 THE SCENE: An accountant has figured that his client owes the government $6,000 in income taxes.

Client's Objective: You'd like your accountant to change some figures on your tax forms so that you won't have to pay that much.

Accountant's Objective: You're a respectable accountant, and you won't do anything dishonest or illegal.

151 THE SCENE: A man in a train station asks a stranger for a dollar so he can get home. It's late at night and only two people are in the train station.

First Man's Objective: You need to get home. Beg the stranger to give you a dollar.

Second Man's Objective: You think this person is a swindler. Refuse to give him any money.

152 THE SCENE: A lawyer is talking to a client about what plea to enter at his upcoming murder trial.

Lawyer's Objective: Talk your client into pleading guilty to manslaughter, rather than pleading not guilty to murder and risking a murder conviction.

Client's Objective: You don't want to plead guilty to anything because you maintain that you didn't kill anyone.

153 THE SCENE: Two people are walking along a path in the woods when they come upon a fork in the road.

First Person's Objective: Your favorite poem is "The Road Not Taken." You want to take the road that looks less traveled.

Second Person's Objective: You never read "The Road Not Taken." Suggest to your companion that it makes more sense to take the road that looks like it has been used more often.

154 THE SCENE: A photographer is snapping pictures of his model during a modeling session.

Model's Objective: You don't like this photographer, and you refuse to smile.

Photographer's Objective: This model is being extremely uncooperative; she refuses to smile. Threaten to fire her if she doesn't cooperate with you.

155 THE SCENE: Two friends planning a vacation together are trying to decide whether to fly or take a train to their destination.

First Friend's Objective: You want to fly because it's faster and more convenient.

Second Friend's Objective: You want to take the train because it's more economical.

156 THE SCENE: Two strangers in a video store want to rent *Casablanca*, but the store only has one copy.

First Person's Objective: You promised your family that you would bring home *Casablanca*. You must have it!

Second Person's Objective: You have a date waiting at home who wants to see *Casablanca*. You must have it!

157 THE SCENE: A teenage boy asks a mail carrier to give him a letter that he is about to deliver to his girlfriend's house.

Boy's Objective: You wrote a letter to your girlfriend accusing her of dating another guy behind your back. You later found out that this wasn't true, but only after you mailed your letter. You know that if the letter goes inside the mail slot on the door, you won't be able to get to it. You must have it!

Mail Carrier's Objective: It's against the law to deliver mail to any person other than the one to whom the letter is addressed. Don't give that letter to the boy.

158 THE SCENE: A man on the street collecting money for a fund for orphans stops a passerby to ask for a donation.

Money Collector's Objective: You'd like to make a lot of money today for the orphan's fund; you were an orphan yourself.

Passerby's Objective: You'd like to contribute, but you need to be convinced that this charity is legitimate.

159 THE SCENE: A man knocks on the door of a stranger's house to ask if he can go inside and use his phone. No other houses are in the area.

Man's Objective: Your car broke down and you need to call a garage.

Homeowner's Objective: You don't trust this man; you think he might rob you if you let him in.

160 THE SCENE: A woman in a department store has lost her five-year-old son and asks the store's security guard to help her find him.

Mother's Objective: You're in a panic; you're afraid that something awful has happened to your son. You must find him immediately!

Security Guard's Objective: You want to do everything you can to help this woman.

THE SCENE: Two friends are in a restaurant enjoying a leisurely meal when one of them suggests that they leave.

First Friend's Objective: You have five minutes to get your friend to a surprise birthday party that's being given in his honor.

Second Friend's Objective: You're having a nice time in the restaurant and you don't want to leave.

162 **THE SCENE:** A man is complaining to his dry cleaner about the way he laundered his shirt.

Man's Objective: You insist that the dry cleaner shrunk your shirt. Demand that he pay for a new shirt.

Dry Cleaner's Objective: Convince the man that you are not responsible for any damage that's been done to his shirt. For all you know, some other dry cleaner could have caused the problem.

163 **THE SCENE:** A librarian is talking to a man about a book that was taken out on his library card.

Librarian's Objective: The book in question is two months overdue. Insist that the man either return the book and pay the overdue fine, or pay twenty dollars for a replacement copy.

Man's Objective: You insist that you never even borrowed the book. Convince the librarian that there is some mistake.

164 **THE SCENE:** A prisoner is talking to his cellmate about his plan to escape.

First Prisoner's Objective: You want to escape, and you want your cellmate to help you.

Second Prisoner's Objective: You don't want to have anything to do with your cellmate's plan to escape. You're up for parole in a few months, and you don't want to get into any trouble now.

165 THE SCENE: A mechanic gives a customer a $500 estimate on the repairs needed for his car.

Customer's Objective: You think the estimate is much too high, and you don't intend to get ripped off by this mechanic.

Mechanic's Objective: You insist that $500 is a fair estimate for the work that's needed to repair the car.

166 THE SCENE: An astronomer is talking to a colleague about a new discovery that he made last night.

First Astronomer's Objective: You're sure that you discovered a new comet last night.

Second Astronomer's Objective: You think that all your colleague saw was some dust on the lens of the telescope.

167 THE SCENE: Two campers are sitting in the middle of the woods late at night before a campfire when one of them thinks he hears an unusual noise.

First Camper's Objective: You think that you hear a large animal approaching, perhaps a bear or a mountain lion. You suggest a hasty retreat.

Second Camper's Objective: You don't hear anything. You think that your friend is imagining things.

168 THE SCENE: A palm reader is examining a man's palm.

Man's Objective: You're interested in finding out what this palm reader can tell you about your future.

Palm Reader's Objective: You've noticed a very short life line on this man, and you're reluctant to tell him that he doesn't have very long to live.

169 THE SCENE: The subject of a portrait is talking to the artist about the finished portrait.

Subject's Objective: You don't think the painting looks like you at all, and you want the artist either to paint it over or to give you your money back.

Artist's Objective: You feel that you've painted a perfect likeness of the subject. Convince the subject that no other artist could paint him any better than you did.

170 THE SCENE: A mortgage banker has just informed an applicant that his request for a loan has been denied.

Applicant's Objective: You've fallen in love with a house that you desperately want. Convince the banker to process your loan.

Banker's Objective: This applicant's credit report shows a history of delinquent payments, and you just can't take a chance on him.

171 THE SCENE: An interior decorator is speaking to a client about how to redecorate a living room.

Decorator's Objective: In order to do what you'd like to do with this room, you need to spend at least $2,000. Talk your client into spending at least that much money.

Client's Objective: You want your living room to look nice, but you're on a strict budget. You can't afford to spend any more than $1,000 to decorate this room. Convince the decorator to do the job for that amount of money.

172 THE SCENE: A passenger is talking to his limousine driver about the best route to take to the airport.

Limousine Driver's Objective: You think that the highway is the best way to the airport. Persuade your passenger to agree to that route.

Passenger's Objective: Persuade your driver to use the back roads; you think they will provide the best route to the airport.

173 THE SCENE: A new barber is giving a haircut to his first customer.

Barber's Objective: You're very nervous, and you want this haircut to be perfect.

Customer's Objective: You're very particular about your hair, and you want it cut perfectly.

174 THE SCENE: A man is talking to an insurance salesman about a life insurance policy.

Man's Objective: You think it's important to have life insurance, but you don't want to pay a premium of more than $100 a month.

Insurance Salesman's Objective: You want this customer to buy a $200-a-month policy.

175 THE SCENE: A very nervous passenger walks into the cockpit of a jet and orders everyone out except the pilot.

Passenger's Objective: You're a hijacker, and you demand that the pilot fly the plane to South America. You have a gun.

Pilot's Objective: Get this passenger to calm down and go back to his seat.

176 THE SCENE: A woman is in a nail salon having her nails done by a manicurist.

Woman's Objective: You haven't been to this nail salon in a while, and you'd like to catch up on all the gossip.

Manicurist's Objective: You're anxious to tell this woman a juicy story about one of your other customers who is having an affair with a married man.

177 THE SCENE: A market research interviewer stops a shopper in a shopping mall and asks if he'd like to participate in a survey on the public's eating habits.

Interviewer's Objective: Every single person you've stopped so far has refused to sit for an interview. You desperately want someone to interview.

Shopper's Objective: You're in a hurry. You don't have time to sit for an interview.

178 THE SCENE: A father is interviewing a prospective nanny for his three-year-old daughter.

Father's Objective: You're looking for the perfect nanny for your daughter, so you ask many specific questions about this person's background and experience.

Nanny's Objective: You want this job desperately; you've been out of work for quite some time. You're also very confident about your ability to care for a young child.

179 THE SCENE: A church organist is speaking to the parish's pastor about the type of music that he'd like to play.

Organist's Objective: You like modern music, so you want the pastor to approve your selection of contemporary liturgical hymns.

Pastor's Objective: You like traditional music, and you only want that kind of music played in your church.

180 THE SCENE: A stockbroker is giving financial advice to a client.

Stockbroker's Objective: Advise your client to buy as many shares of Badbyte Computer Company stock as he can afford. You're sure that it will double in value by the end of the month.

Client's Objective: A friend of yours who uses the same stockbroker called yesterday to warn you. The broker gave your friend some very bad advice, which resulted in your friend losing thousands of dollars. Therefore, you're not so willing to listen to this broker.

181 THE SCENE: A pharmacist is talking to a customer about a prescription for tranquilizers that he'd like filled.

Pharmacist's Objective: The prescription is an obvious fake. Keep the man occupied until you can call the police.

Customer's Objective: Your prescription is fake. You want the tranquilizers so that you can sell them illegally on the street.

182 THE SCENE: A man pulls aside a beauty contest judge just before he's about to take some time to think about whom he'd like to choose as the contest's winner.

Man's Objective: You want your girlfriend to win the contest. Offer the judge some money to give your girlfriend first prize.

Judge's Objective: You're an essentially honest person, but you are occasionally tempted to do something that's unethical or immoral if there's something in it for you.

183 THE SCENE: A patient who has been waiting for an hour and a half to see his doctor is questioning the doctor's receptionist.

Patient's Objective: You're angry because you've been waiting a very long time. Demand to know why you've had to wait so long.

Receptionist's Objective: The patient has been waiting for a long time because the doctor is very busy. Calm the patient down and explain to him why he's had to wait so long.

184 THE SCENE: A boxer is working out with his trainer. He's been exercising and lifting weights for the last hour and a half.

Boxer's Objective: You're dead tired, and you want to quit.

Trainer's Objective: Insist that the boxer work out for another half hour.

185 **THE SCENE:** The security guard in a jewelry store stops a customer and asks to look inside his jacket.

Security Guard's Objective: You think that you saw the customer take a gold bracelet and put it inside his jacket. Demand to see what's inside the customer's jacket.

Customer's Objective: You stole a gold bracelet and put it in the inside pocket of your jacket. Of course, you don't want anyone to know about it.

186 **THE SCENE:** A man has just tried to adjust his friend's neck after his friend complained of a stiff neck. But instead of making his neck feel better, it now feels worse than it did before.

First Man's Objective: You think that if you tug at his neck again, you can fix it right this time. Convince him to give you another chance.

Second Man's Objective: You don't want to take any more chances with amateur chiropractors. Don't let anyone but a qualified doctor touch your neck.

187 **THE SCENE:** A soldier is talking to his sergeant about searching for his friend who's been lost on the battlefield.

Soldier's Objective: Insist that you be given a few hours to try to find your friend.

Sergeant's Objective: Refuse to let the soldier go; it's too dangerous.

188 **THE SCENE:** Two people walk into the laundry room of an apartment building and see only one unused washing machine.

First Person's Objective: You insist that you saw the machine first and you should have first use of it.

Second Person's Objective: You insist that you saw the machine first and you should have first use of it.

189 **THE SCENE:** A prisoner in a jail cell is talking to his jailer.

Prisoner's Objective: Convince the jailer that you know lots of people on the outside who would pay him thousands of dollars if he lets you escape.

Jailer's Objective: You're tired of listening to this prisoner; you want him to shut his mouth.

190 **THE SCENE:** A candidate running for Congress is talking to his campaign manager about going public about his experiences smoking marijuana when he was in college.

Candidate's Objective: You feel that if this news comes out before you have a chance to make it public yourself, you won't have a chance of winning the election.

Campaign Manager's Objective: You think that the candidate should take his chances and keep his mouth shut about what he did in college. You feel that the odds are in his favor.

191 **THE SCENE:** An investigative news reporter is questioning a U.S. senator about his participation in a bribery scandal.

Reporter's Objective: You think that the senator is guilty, and you'd like to trick him into admitting his participation in the scandal.

Senator's Objective: Insist that you were never involved in the scandal.

192 **THE SCENE:** A man is talking to a psychologist about a recurring nightmare that he's been having for the past week or so. He's been dreaming about falling off a cliff. The psychologist believes that he's having the dream because he's feeling guilty about something.

Man's Objective: You think that the psychologist is wrong because you can't think of anything you feel guilty about.

Psychologist's Objective: You're sure that your interpretation of the dream is correct. Question the man until you discover the cause of the guilt.

193 **THE SCENE:** A private investigator is telling a client that he could find no evidence to prove that his wife has been cheating on him.

Private Investigator's Objective: Convince the client that he's wrong about his wife; she hasn't been cheating on him.

Client's Objective: Demand that he continue to investigate your wife; you're sure that she's having an affair.

194 **THE SCENE:** A man is talking to a coat check boy about some money that's been taken from his coat.

Man's Objective: You think the coat check boy stole the money. Threaten to call the police if he doesn't return it.

Boy's Objective: You didn't take any money. Plead your innocence.

195 **THE SCENE:** An actor is talking to his director about the interpretation of his role.

Actor's Objective: You think that the character you're playing is naive and immature. Defend your interpretation.

Director's Objective: You think that the actor's character is a conniving sneak, and that he's only pretending to be naive. Defend your interpretation.

196 **THE SCENE:** Two American astronauts are about to be the first humans to land on Mars. They're trying to decide what will go down in history as the first words spoken on the surface of Mars.

First Astronaut's Objective: You believe the first words spoken on Mars should be, "We come in peace for all mankind."

Second Astronaut's Objective: You believe the first words spoken on Mars should be, "We come in peace for all Americans."

197 **THE SCENE:** Two strangers are about to get in the same taxi cab.

First Person's Objective: You insist that you saw the cab first and that it's yours.

Second Person's Objective: You insist that you saw the cab first and that it's yours.

198 **THE SCENE:** A homeowner mentions to a teenage neighbor that he will be going on vacation next week and needs someone to water his lawn while he's away.

Homeowner's Objective: You're sorry that you said anything because you didn't mean to suggest to your teenage neighbor that you'd like him to take care of your lawn. The fact is you don't trust him.

Neighbor's Objective: Offer to take care of your neighbor's lawn.

199 **THE SCENE:** A gardener is explaining to a homeowner that poinsettias won't grow in his New England home's garden.

Homeowner's Objective: You're sure that poinsettias will grow in your climate. Order your gardener to plant them.

Gardener's Objective: Explain that poinsettias are a tropical plant that can't possibly grow in New England.

200 **THE SCENE:** A prospective college student is discussing his high school transcript with a college interviewer.

Interviewer's Objective: You'd like to know why this student did so well during the first three marking periods of his senior year, but failed almost every subject in his last marking period.

Student's Objective: Try to convince the interviewer that you weren't slacking off in your last marking period. Get him to buy the idea that you failed almost every subject that marking period because you became ill.

2

Using Contrasts

Neil Simon discovered that if you take a character who is hopelessly sloppy and have him live with a neatness fanatic, the possibilities for a play are almost endless. In fact, enough situations resulted from this combination of character types to keep "The Odd Couple" television series going for several years. Think of some popular plays, films, and TV shows. How many of them involve leading characters that have diametrically opposed personalities?

The improvisation starters in this chapter provide conflicting character traits and emotions as a means to begin improvisations. The instructor should simply have the players take the stage, and then read aloud the scene and character descriptions for each player. The players should immediately begin at this point. Remind your players of the same rules described in Chapter 1, with the addition of the following: everything you do and say should be consistent with your character's personality or emotional state, but avoid stereotypes. There is more than one way to express shyness, anxiety, frustration, elation, etc. Each person is unique; don't use clichéd means of expressing your character.

You may use the following guide questions when discussing the performances with your players and audience:

1. What specific conflicts resulted from the contrasting character traits, emotions, attitudes, or moods portrayed by the players?

2. Did the players *talk* about their characteristics, or did they *show* that they possessed them? Did you notice any specific vocal or visible adjustments that were made to communicate their characteristics?

3. Did the players' traits, emotions, moods, and attitudes seem honest and natural, or were they playing stereotypes?

4. Did the improvisation develop as you expected, or were you surprised by the direction in which it turned?

 THE SCENE: Two patients are waiting in a dentist's waiting room.

Player One: You're relaxed. You have no major dental problems, and you're only seeing the dentist for a routine checkup.

Player Two: You're nervous. You haven't been to the dentist in years, and you expect to have a mouthful of cavities to be drilled.

 THE SCENE: Two students are comparing each other's report cards.

Player One: You're stupid. You've failed every subject, even gym.

Player Two: You're intelligent. You've earned A's in every subject, including calculus, organic chemistry, and Russian literature.

 THE SCENE: Two friends are watching a film in a movie theater.

Player One: You're very excited during a very suspenseful part of a movie.

Player Two: You're calm. You've seen this movie twice before and you know what is about to happen.

 THE SCENE: Two award nominees are sitting at a table at a theatrical awards ceremony.

Player One: You're confident. You've been nominated for an award, and you just know you will win it.

Player Two: You lack confidence. You've been nominated for the same award, but you're sure it won't go to you.

5 THE SCENE: Two passersby are outside a bank where robbers are holding the bank tellers hostage.

Player One: You're heroic. You want to sneak into the building and try to free the hostages.

Player Two: You're unheroic. You want to stay as far as possible from the bank.

6 THE SCENE: Two gamblers are seated at a blackjack table in a gambling casino.

Player One: You're angry. You just lost $500 playing blackjack.

Player Two: You're ecstatic. You just won $500 playing at the same table.

7 THE SCENE: Two friends are walking along a street in a big city.

Player One: You're naive. You see some guys across the street selling watches, and you think you can get a good deal on one.

Player Two: You're streetwise. You realize that those watches are probably stolen.

8 THE SCENE: Two friends are at a party.

Player One: You're conceited. You think everyone at the party is looking at you because they think you're incredibly attractive.

Player Two: You're insecure. You think everyone is looking at you because they think you're incredibly ugly.

9 THE SCENE: Two college roommates are in a messy dormitory room.

Player One: You're lazy. You don't want to waste your energy cleaning up the room. All you want to do is sit and watch television.

Player Two: You're energetic. You want to clean up the room and then go jogging.

10 **THE SCENE:** Two guys are standing on a corner watching girls walk by.

Player One: You're rude. Your humor is crude, and your comments about the passing women are tasteless.

Player Two: You're courteous. You object to your partner's descriptions and comments.

11 **THE SCENE:** A husband and wife are visiting a house that's for sale.

Player One: You're hypercritical. You find fault with just about everything in this house.

Player Two: You're not very discriminating. You think the house is just fine.

12 **THE SCENE:** Two friends are watching a football game on television.

Player One: You're upset. Your team is losing the game.

Player Two: You're overjoyed. Your team is winning the game.

13 **THE SCENE:** Two friends are walking along a road.

Player One: You're suspicious. You've found a wrapped package in the middle of the road with a sign that says "Open Me" attached to it. You think it might be a bomb or something.

Player Two: You're trusting. You think some generous person has left a gift for some lucky person to find.

14 **THE SCENE:** Two people are looking at an abstract painting in an art gallery.

Player One: You're very insightful. You see in this painting a symbolic representation of man's inhumanity to man.

Player Two: You're superficial. You see nothing but a chaotic arrangement of shapes and colors.

15 THE SCENE: Two painters are painting a room.

Player One: You're an experienced painter. You know exactly what you're doing.

Player Two: You're an inexperienced painter. You don't know what you're doing.

16 THE SCENE: Two friends are leaving a movie theater after seeing an action-adventure film.

Player One: You thought the movie was great. You were also very impressed by the acting in the film.

Player Two: You thought the movie was awful. You can't believe that the actors in the film are making a living as actors.

17 THE SCENE: Two teenage brothers or sisters (or a brother and sister) are clearing the dining room table after dinner.

Player One: You work very quickly and efficiently. You'd like to get this done so that you can go out to meet your friends.

Player Two: You work very slowly. You have nothing to do, so you're in no rush.

18 THE SCENE: Two friends are sitting inside a beach house because it's raining.

Player One: You're optimistic. You're sure that it will soon stop raining and you will be able to hit the beach.

Player Two: You're pessimistic. You think that you will be stuck inside all day.

19 THE SCENE: Two hosts of a party have just said good-bye to their last guest. It's two o'clock in the morning.

Player One: You're exhausted. You'd like to go to bed now and leave the mess until tomorrow.

Player Two: You're wide awake. You want to clean up everything now, and then watch some television!

20 THE SCENE: Two students are in a high school corridor waiting for English class to begin.

Player One: You love English. You can't wait to go inside and continue your studies of Chaucer.

Player Two: You hate English, and you find no value in the study of Chaucer.

21 THE SCENE: A tennis player is complaining to a line judge about the judge's "out" call on his second serve.

Player One: You're a hot-tempered tennis player. You believe the serve was "in." You vehemently express your opinion and question the judge's competence.

Player Two: You are a very professional and unemotional line judge. You calmly explain how you saw the call, and you're not affected by the tennis player's abrasive behavior.

22 THE SCENE: Two friends are resting after jogging two miles.

Player One: You are terribly out of shape; you can't take another step.

Player Two: You are in great shape; you're ready to go another couple of miles.

23 THE SCENE: Two brothers or sisters are trying to decide how to decorate a room that they will share.

Player One: You have modern taste. You'd like to decorate the room with abstract posters and bright colors.

Player Two: You have conservative taste. You'd like to decorate the room with traditional prints of landscape paintings.

 THE SCENE: Two friends are standing by the side of a frozen lake on a cold winter's day.

Player One: You're adventurous and daring. You'd like to walk across the lake even though a sign is posted that says, "Danger — Thin Ice."

Player Two: You'd rather be safe than sorry. You refuse to take one step on the ice.

25 THE SCENE: Two people are at a bus stop waiting for a bus.

Player One: You're very impatient. The bus is five minutes late and this annoys you.

Player Two: You're perfectly content. You're sure the bus will arrive at any moment.

26 THE SCENE: Two friends are walking along a road when a black cat crosses their path.

Player One: You're superstitious. You're sure that something terrible will happen to you today.

Player Two: You're a realist. You believe all that nonsense about black cats is ridiculous.

27 THE SCENE: Two brothers or sisters (or a brother and sister) walk into the living room of their house and find a large box on the floor.

Player One: You're curious. You'd like to open the box and see what's inside it.

Player Two: You're not concerned about the contents of the box. You think that you should leave it alone; it's not yours to open.

28 THE SCENE: Two high school football players are in a locker room.

Player One: You're quick-tempered. You heard that a player from a rival team has been saying nasty things about your team. You want to find this person and let him have it.

Player Two: You're a peaceful person. You think it's best just to let it slide.

29 THE SCENE: Two teenage brothers or sisters (or a brother and sister) are talking to each other after they've been scolded by their parents for coming home at two o'clock in the morning.

Player One: You're disrespectful. You complain that your parents are a couple of old fogies who should mind their own business.

Player Two: You're respectful. You're sorry for coming home so late and you think your parents have every right to be angry with you.

30 THE SCENE: Two students are in a library working together on a research paper.

Player One: You're dishonest. You think it's okay to make up a few book titles to include in your bibliography so that it will appear that you've done more research than you actually did. You also don't mind including a few phony footnotes throughout the paper.

Player Two: You're honest. You wouldn't dream of using any fake books or footnotes.

31 THE SCENE: Two teenage friends are discussing the respective dates they went on last night.

Player One: You have traditional values. You believe that men should open doors for women, and that the man should always pay.

Player Two: You have modern values. You believe in women's liberation.

32 THE SCENE: Two friends are discussing the date that one of the two went on last night.

Player One: You're very nosy. You want to hear all the details of your friend's date.

Player Two: You're secretive. You're not willing to divulge too much information.

33 THE SCENE: Two friends are sitting at a table in a restaurant eating lunch.

Player One: You're very talkative. You speak very quickly, and you don't give your friend much chance to get a word in edgewise.

Player Two: You're very quiet. You mostly nod your head and react nonverbally to what your friend says.

34 THE SCENE: Two students are leaving a classroom after getting back a test that they both failed.

Player One: You're shocked. You thought you did much better on this test.

Player Two: You're not surprised at all. You expected a failing grade.

35 THE SCENE: Two friends at a campsite are sitting before a campfire.

Player One: You love camping. You're having a wonderful time.

Player Two: You hate camping and everything about it. You'd rather be indoors.

36 THE SCENE: Two friends are at a rock concert.

Player One: You love rock music. You're having a great time.

Player Two: You hate rock music. You can't wait to leave.

37 THE SCENE: Two friends are at a party in a buffet dinner line.

Player One: You're ravenous. You help yourself to huge portions of everything you see.

Player Two: You're full. You ate before the party because you didn't know that food would be served.

38 **THE SCENE:** Two friends are taking turns playing pinball.

Player One: You play very aggressively. You're determined to beat the high score that's listed on the machine.

Player Two: You're a passive player. You are really not very interested in the game; you're just playing to pass the time.

39 **THE SCENE:** Two doubles partners are playing tennis.

Player One: You are extremely assertive. You want to make sure that the match is played exactly the way you have in mind, so you give your partner exact instructions that must be followed.

Player Two: You are submissive. You do everything that your partner tells you to do.

40 **THE SCENE:** A prospective college student is being interviewed by a college official.

Player One: You, as the interviewer, are very formal and professional in your manner.

Player Two: You, as the interviewee, are inappropriately informal in your manner. You make light of the entire interview.

41 **THE SCENE:** A man and a woman at a party have just been introduced.

Player One: You are bold. You make it clear that you're attracted to this person.

Player Two: You are shy. You're not used to such aggressive behavior.

42 **THE SCENE:** Two private investigators are searching a room, trying to find evidence to use against a client's husband, whom she believes is cheating on her.

Player One: You're anxious. You want to get out of the room as soon as possible because you think your client's husband will arrive at any moment.

Player Two: You're taking your sweet time. You believe that the husband won't show up for hours.

43 THE SCENE: Two friends are watching a movie on television.

Player One: You're laughing uncontrollably. You think the movie is hysterical!

Player Two: You're bored. You think the movie is ridiculous and unfunny.

44 THE SCENE: Two friends are eating dinner at a fancy restaurant.

Player One: You're well-bred. Your manners are extremely refined.

Player Two: You're uncultured. You behave like a slob.

45 THE SCENE: Two high school students have just left the principal's office after being reprimanded for smoking in the bathroom.

Player One: You're repentant. You're very sorry for what you did, and you swear that you will never do it again.

Player Two: You're not sorry at all for what you did. You only regret being caught. You swear that next time you will be more careful.

46 THE SCENE: Two brothers or sisters (or a brother and a sister) are polishing and waxing the family car.

Player One: You're meticulous. You're very careful about the way you shine every square inch of this car.

Player Two: You're careless. You want to get the job done as quickly as possible, and you don't care how it looks when you're finished.

THE SCENE: Two friends are discussing the value of a college education.

Player One: You're open-minded. You think that some people may be better off getting a job immediately after high school.

Player Two: You're narrow-minded. You insist that all people will benefit from a college education.

 THE SCENE: Two chefs are in a restaurant preparing a stew.

Player One: You're an experienced chef. You know exactly how to prepare this meal; you've done it hundreds of times before.

Player Two: This is your first day as a chef. You don't know what you're doing, but you don't want the other chef to know that.

THE SCENE: Two students are in a classroom taking a mathematics test.

Player One: You're sneaky. You try every way you can think of to cheat, including taking peeks at the other student's test paper.

Player Two: You're honest. You would never dream of cheating on a test, and you won't allow others to use you to cheat either.

 THE SCENE: Two patients are sitting in a doctor's office waiting to see the doctor for their annual physical examinations.

Player One: You're a hypochondriac. You believe you have every illness known to man.

Player Two: You believe that you are a model of perfect health.

THE SCENE: Two adults are playing with a one-year-old baby boy.

Player One: You feel secure with the child. Even though you are careful not to hurt the baby, you enjoy tossing him in the air and catching him.

Player Two: You are not comfortable with this child. You are afraid of hurting him.

52 THE SCENE: Two teens are dancing at a party.

Player One: You're very relaxed on the dance floor.

Player Two: You're very stiff on the dance floor. Your movements are sharp and mechanical; you feel extremely uncomfortable.

53 THE SCENE: Two high school students are at their senior prom, checking their appearance in a rest room mirror.

Player One: You're vain. You think that you're the best-looking one at the prom. You believe everyone admires you and wants to be just like you.

Player Two: You have a serious lack of self-confidence. You think that you're ugly and worthless, and that your date is having an awful time.

54 THE SCENE: A teenager notices that a friend's fly is unzipped.

Player One: You think this is the funniest thing that you've every seen. You can't stop laughing!

Player Two: You don't see any humor in this. You think that your friend is being extremely immature.

55 THE SCENE: Two brothers or sisters (or a brother and sister) are having breakfast at seven o'clock A.M.

Player One: You're grouchy. You're always cranky this early in the morning.

Player Two: You're cheerful. You've already been up for an hour, and you're looking forward to a great day.

56 **THE SCENE:** Two friends are standing in front of a movie theater waiting for a third friend to arrive.

Player One: You're extremely annoyed. The movie will begin in five minutes, and the person you're waiting for is already ten minutes late.

Player Two: You're calm. You're confident that the person you're waiting for will show up in time for the movie.

57 **THE SCENE:** Two workers are digging ditches on a very hot day.

Player One: You're exhausted. You don't know how much more of this you can take.

Player Two: You're in fine shape. You can go on working for hours.

58 **THE SCENE:** Two friends are stopped on a Ferris wheel at the very top.

Player One: You're scared to death. You hate heights; the only reason you agreed to go on this ride was that your friend begged you to go.

Player Two: You're having a wonderful time. You enjoy waving your hands wildly and rocking the car.

59 **THE SCENE:** Two people are about to participate in a pie-eating contest.

Player One: You can't wait to dig in! You won this contest last year, and you plan to recapture the title this year.

Player Two: The thought of doing this is making you sick. You only agreed to participate in this contest because you lost a bet.

60 **THE SCENE:** A beggar stops a person on the street and asks for money.

Player One: You are a homeless beggar. You don't have a penny to your name, and you need money to eat.

Player Two: You are quite wealthy, and you don't like being bothered by street beggars.

61 THE SCENE: Two people are sitting in the lobby of an accounting firm, waiting to be interviewed for a position as an accountant.

Player One: You have high self-esteem. You're sure that the position will go to you.

Player Two: You have low self-esteem. You're sure that you will be turned down.

62 THE SCENE: Two friends are sitting in a living room watching an arty foreign film on television.

Player One: You're very knowledgeable about film making. You notice specific techniques involving camera angles, the use of shadows, symbolism, etc.

Player Two: You know absolutely nothing about cinematography, and what's more, you don't understand what your friend is talking about.

63 THE SCENE: Two friends are trying to decide where to go for dinner.

Player One: You have expensive taste. You want to go to "La Dolce Vita," an elegant Italian restaurant.

Player Two: You have casual taste. You want to go to "Rudy's House of Ribs," a very informal and inexpensive restaurant.

64 THE SCENE: Two high school seniors are waiting in the principal's office for the principal to arrive.

Player One: You are a model student, and you're frightened. You don't know why you've been called to the principal's office, but you fear it's because you did something wrong.

Player Two: You're the school's number one troublemaker. You're not intimidated by the principal; you're used to this.

65 **THE SCENE:** Two friends are walking through a park on a sunny day.

Player One: You love the sun. You think a dark tan makes you look healthy; you'd like to sit on a bench or lie on a blanket and take in some rays.

Player Two: You hate the sun. You're afraid of developing skin cancer from exposure to dangerous ultraviolet rays; you suggest sitting in a shaded area.

66 **THE SCENE:** A husband and wife are sitting in the living room of their house on a hot summer afternoon.

Player One: You're economical. You don't want to turn on the air conditioner because it's too expensive to operate.

Player Two: You don't care about the cost. You want to set the air conditioner to its highest setting.

67 **THE SCENE:** A husband and wife are looking through travel brochures trying to decide where to spend their vacation.

Player One: You love the outdoors. You'd like to spend a week camping and hiking in the mountains.

Player Two: You love big cities. You'd like to spend a week in New York City or Los Angeles.

68 **THE SCENE:** Two convicts are sitting in a prison cell.

Player One: You're domineering. You threaten to kill your cellmate if he doesn't obey your every order.

Player Two: You're meek. You do everything your cellmate tells you to do without hesitation.

 THE SCENE: Two teenage brothers or sisters (or a brother and sister) are sitting at home alone late at night.

Player One: You're jumpy. You react to every little sound that you hear.

Player Two: You're not at all bothered by the sounds. You think your brother (or sister) is imagining all these noises.

70 **THE SCENE:** Two high school students find out they received a grade of "D" on an English class research project that they worked on together.

Player One: You think that you're perfect. You place the blame for the poor grade entirely on your partner.

Player Two: You have a poor self-image. You take full responsibility for the grade.

71 **THE SCENE:** Two friends are sitting at a table in a quiet library doing some schoolwork.

Player One: Your voice is very loud. The librarian has asked you to lower your voice several times, but you have paid little attention to her.

Player Two: Your voice is very soft. You are embarrassed by your friend's loud voice.

72 **THE SCENE:** Two friends are sitting in a restaurant waiting for a meal they've ordered to be served.

Player One: You're impatient. You ordered the meal twenty minutes ago and you feel it should have been served by now.

Player Two: You're patient. You realize that the restaurant is very busy and that it may take longer than usual for your meal to be served.

73 **THE SCENE:** Two college students are discussing their post-graduation plans.

Player One: You're very practical. You believe that you should waste no time looking for a job. You'd like to be employed before the summer is over.

Player Two: You're impractical. You'd like to travel around Europe for a while before looking for a job, even though you have no idea where you will get the money to do this.

74 THE SCENE: Two friends are playing a ring toss game at a carnival.

Player One: You're determined to win a huge stuffed teddy bear, but in order to do that, you have to score three "ringers" in a row. Three tosses of the ring cost fifty cents, and you've already spent nine dollars on this game.

Player Two: You give up easily. You tried the game once, and now you want to move on to another game.

75 THE SCENE: Two friends have just left a clothing store in a shopping mall when they notice that they were under charged for their purchases.

Player One: You're honest. You want to go back inside the store and pay them for the amount that you were undercharged.

Player Two: You're dishonest. You want to hurry on home before someone realizes the mistake and comes after you.

76 THE SCENE: Two friends are in a theater watching a romantic film.

Player One: You're extremely emotional. You cry throughout the entire film.

Player Two: You're unemotional. You're not moved by what's going on in the film.

77 THE SCENE: Two athletes are lifting weights in a gym.

Player One: You're weak. You can hardly lift the lightest weights.

Player Two: You're strong. You can lift the heaviest weights effortlessly.

78 THE SCENE: Two strangers meet at a party.

Player One: You're friendly. You'd like to get to know this person better.

Player Two: You're unfriendly. You don't feel much like talking.

79 **THE SCENE:** Two friends are discussing the fishing trip that they went on last week.

Player One: You're a braggart. You can't stop praising yourself for how many fish you caught.

Player Two: You're modest. You caught the same number of fish as your partner, but you're not so impressed with yourself.

80 **THE SCENE:** Two friends are making plans for dinner.

Player One: You'd like to go to a seafood restaurant, but you're willing to compromise.

Player Two: You're not willing to compromise. You want Chinese food or nothing.

81 **THE SCENE:** Two students are in a library studying.

Player One: Your level of concentration is very high. You're completely focused on your work.

Player Two: You're very distracted by every little thing that's happening around you. You can't stay focused on your work for more than a few seconds at a time.

82 **THE SCENE:** Two students are discussing their new teacher.

Player One: You're mean and nasty. You don't have one nice thing to say about the teacher.

Player Two: You're very kind. You give the teacher the benefit of every doubt.

83 THE SCENE: Two friends are at a roulette wheel in a gambling casino.

Player One: You love to take risks. You want to bet large sums of money on single numbers.

Player Two: You like to play it safe. You'd rather place small bets on the red and black squares.

84 THE SCENE: Two friends are spending the day in an amusement park.

Player One: You're thrilled to be here. You want to go on every ride twice.

Player Two: You're bored to tears. You want to leave.

85 THE SCENE: Two friends are lying out on the beach.

Player One: You're very comfortable. You love the sun; you can stay on the beach all day.

Player Two: You're very uncomfortable. You're hot and sweaty and you'd rather be in an air-conditioned room.

86 THE SCENE: Two friends are shopping in a clothing store.

Player One: You're a spendthrift. You want to buy practically everything you see without concern for the cost.

Player Two: You're thrifty. You look for bargains.

87 THE SCENE: Two people are working in the same office when the phone rings. A stranger has called to say that a bomb has been planted in their office, and it is scheduled to go off any second now.

Player One: You're undaunted. You think this is a prank call.

Player Two: You're very frightened; you take the call very seriously.

THE SCENE: A married couple is trying to decide how much they should donate to a certain charitable organization.

Player One: You're very charitable. You want to donate $500.

Player Two: You're uncharitable. You don't want to contribute anything to this charity.

 THE SCENE: Two friends are discussing a mutual friend who was arrested for assault.

Player One: You're sympathetic. You think your friend must have had a good reason to do what he did.

Player Two: You're unsympathetic. You think your friend is a hothead and got what he deserved.

THE SCENE: Two brothers or sisters (or a brother and sister) are working in their garden planting flowers.

Player One: You don't like getting your hands dirty. You make a great effort to stay clean.

Player Two: You don't mind getting dirt under your fingernails.

THE SCENE: Two students are sitting in a library doing their homework.

Player One: You're very frustrated. This homework assignment is very difficult for you.

Player Two: You're perfectly relaxed. This homework assignment is a breeze for you.

THE SCENE: Two people have been trapped for an hour in an elevator that is stuck between floors.

Player One: You're hopeful that someone will come to rescue you soon.

Player Two: You're disheartened. You think that you will be stuck in the elevator all day.

93 **THE SCENE:** A husband and wife are figuring out their income taxes for the year.

Player One: You're concerned about the amount of money that you may have to pay the IRS. You don't know if you can afford it.

Player Two: You're unconcerned. You're sure that you will be able to afford any amount of money that you may owe the government.

94 **THE SCENE:** Two softball players are discussing their team's losing streak.

Player One: You're very discouraged. You don't think your team will ever win another game.

Player Two: You're undismayed. You're confident that your team will win your very next game.

95 **THE SCENE:** Two friends are watching a boxing match.

Player One: You're horrified. You think boxing is a barbaric, uncivilized sport that should be outlawed.

Player Two: You're caught up in the excitement of the match; boxing is your favorite sport.

96 **THE SCENE:** Two teenage friends have been paid ten dollars after doing some yard work for a neighbor.

Player One: You're very appreciative of your neighbor's generosity. You didn't expect to be paid that much.

Player Two: You're unappreciative. You think you deserve a lot more than ten dollars for all the work you did.

97 THE SCENE: Two parents are watching their sons play in a game of basketball.

Player One: You're very supportive of your son. You offer encouraging remarks and statements of approval.

Player Two: You're unsupportive. You continually criticize your son for making even the smallest mistakes, and you offer no praise for anything that he does well.

98 THE SCENE: Two brothers or sisters (or a brother and sister) are discussing the lie that they told their parents last night.

Player One: You're filled with guilt. You've never lied to your parents before.

Player Two: Your conscience is clear. You believe that it's perfectly okay to tell a lie every once in a while.

99 THE SCENE: Two friends have just watched a television commercial about a knife that can cut through anything and stay as sharp as new.

Player One: You're trusting. You believe everything you see on television.

Player Two: You're skeptical. You think that the commercial is a hoax.

 100 THE SCENE: Two brothers or sisters (or a brother and sister) are walking to church on a Sunday morning.

Player One: You're very devout. You would never let a Sunday pass without going to church.

Player Two: You're not very religious. You suggest that you hang out in the park for an hour or so, and then go back home and tell your parents that you went to church.

3

Using Obstacles in Solo Improvisations

The leading characters in a good play or film often need to overcome many difficult obstacles before they can accomplish their objectives. Some of these obstacles may be physical, perhaps involving destructive forces of nature, time limitations, or the interference of others. Sometimes the obstacles are psychological, perhaps involving deep-seated guilt or hidden fears. Whatever the type, the obstacles that the characters must confront help create powerful dramatic tension and excitement.

Each improvisation starter in this chapter provides an obstacle that stands in the way of an objective. The player must find a way to overcome this barrier to his or her objective. Some obstacles are physical, some are psychological; all will challenge the player to find a creative solution to his predicament.

The improvisation starters included here are to be performed solo, so that the player can concentrate upon removing his obstruction without the help of another person. This isn't as easily done with the improvisation starters for two players included in the first two chapters of this book. Take, for example, the situation in Chapter 1 involving a teenage boy who needs to get his father's permission to go to a party. Obviously, the teen's father provides the obstacle. The teen may try a few methods of his own to overcome the obstacle. But it may also happen that the father gives his permission because *he* decides that it's all right for him to go — without being influenced by the teen at all! The improvisation starters in this chapter force the player alone to deal with the obstacle. Since no help is available from any other person, the player must find his own solution to his problem.

These solo improvisations are simple to run. The instructor should have the player take the stage or playing area, and then simply read aloud the improvisation starter. The improvisation should then start immediately.

Review the following two guidelines before beginning:

1. Work on overcoming your obstacle throughout the entire improvisation. Try as many ways as you can think of to do this. But be warned, you may find yourself in an impossible situation! Keep at it until you have either overcome your obstacle or your instructor tells you to stop.

2. Don't feel obligated to speak. The improvisation may be performed as a pantomime. Most people don't constantly talk to themselves when they are alone, but some people do like to "think out loud." If speaking out loud helps, then go ahead and do it; but don't do it for the benefit of the audience. If the audience doesn't understand what you're doing, don't worry about it. You can discuss the improvisation with them after it's over.

You may use the following guide questions when discussing the performances with your players and audience:

1. How did the player attempt to overcome the obstacle? Was an original approach used?

2. Did the player clearly understand the objective?

3. What might the player have done differently to overcome the obstacle and accomplish the objective? What do you think you would have done?

4. What was the player's attitude toward the obstacle? What was his mood or emotional state?

1. You're sitting at home alone watching television when you hear a noise coming from the kitchen. It sounds like someone is trying to break into the house through the back kitchen door. You want to call the police, but the only phone in the house is in the kitchen. You try running out of the house, but the lock on the door has been mysteriously bolted from the other side.

2. You're at a business meeting about to give an important speech presentation to a committee. This speech could make or break your career. When you stand to give the speech, you discover that you've lost your voice!

3. You've come home at three o'clock in the morning. You are standing at your front door desperate to go inside because you have to go to the bathroom badly. When you reach inside your pocket to get your keys, you discover that they are missing.

4. While trying to fix a broken vase with instant bonding glue, you've glued your fingers together, making it very difficult for you to dial a phone or open a door. You try pulling your hands apart, but if you pull too hard, you will rip your skin.

5. You're an actor waiting to make your entrance on stage. Your cue to enter comes up in about two minutes. You're drinking a cup of coffee off-stage as you wait. As you take a sip, the cup slips from your hand and you spill coffee all over the front of your costume. Unfortunately, you don't have enough time to change.

6. You're a private investigator about to surreptitiously take some photos of the person you've been following. This will be your last opportunity to take pictures of this person before you have to report to the client who hired you. As you begin to focus your camera, a gust of wind blows a huge quantity of dust into your eyes. You won't be able to see a thing for several minutes, and your subject will be gone at any moment.

7. You're standing at the edge of a lake shoreline. Your friend is in the lake swimming when he gets a cramp and calls to you for help. You want to help him, but you don't know how to swim. No one is around for miles, and you have no rope or buoy to throw to him.

8. You're watching a horror movie on television. A very bloody murder scene is taking place. You want to watch because you're very involved in the movie, but the sight of blood always makes you sick.

9. You're on a strict diet. You've set a goal to lose three pounds this week, and you've already lost two. You open the refrigerator and see one last slice of your mother's homemade cherry cheesecake. You've never been able to resist your mother's cheesecake!

10. You're standing in front of a movie theater's box office about to buy a ticket when you discover that you can't pay the price of admission because you don't have enough money. The friends you were supposed to meet are already inside. You'd like to ask someone for the extra money that you need, but no one is around. Everybody is in the theater; the movie began five minutes ago.

11. You work for a company that does a great deal of business with French clients. One of the reasons you were hired for this job is because you wrote on your résumé that you speak French. However, you lied! You're in your office minutes before a French client is about to meet with you. This client does not speak a word of English.

12. You were asked to meet a date at 6:30 P.M. outside the door of a restaurant that you've never been to before. It's now 6:25 P.M. As you look around, you notice a sign above the door that reads, "Formal Attire Required, Policy Strictly Enforced." You're wearing ripped jeans and a T-shirt.

13. You're a teen just waking up at 10:30 in the morning. Your house is a mess because you threw a wild party last night. When you realize that it's 10:30, you begin to panic. Your parents will be home from their vacation at about eleven o'clock. If they see that you've had a party when they were away, you're dead!

14. You're a student sitting in class listening to your teacher's lecture. The material that the teacher is covering will be on a very important test tomorrow. Unfortunately, you didn't get much sleep last night, and you're struggling to stay awake.

15. You're out in the wilderness camping. All of your food is out, ready to be cooked. You're about to light your campfire when you realize that you forgot to pack a book of matches.

16. You're sitting in a very quiet library. Your mind starts to wander and you begin to think of something hysterically funny that happened to you yesterday. You feel like bursting out with laughter, but you know that if you do you will disturb the people sitting around you.

17. You promised your friend that you would call him tonight. You haven't called him in a week, and you know that if you don't call tonight, he will be very angry with you. When you pick up your phone, you discover that the line is dead. You would see him in person, but your car is in the shop and he lives too far away for you to walk.

18. You're a student whose ten-page research paper is due tomorrow morning. You turn on the switch of your electric typewriter only to discover that it is broken. No other typewriter is in your house, and it's too late at night to try to borrow one from a friend.

19. You're planning to propose to your girlfriend tonight. She will be at your apartment any minute now. You've made sure that everything is perfect — dinner, candles, music, etc. However, when you open the box containing the engagement ring to give it one last shine, you discover that it is gone!

20. You're in a car stopped at a red light when your engine stalls. You try to restart the car, but the engine just won't turn over. You're blocking an intersection, and dozens of angry motorists are behind you waiting for you to move.

21. You're getting ready to go on a very important job interview. As you reach to open a bottom drawer of your dresser, you hurt your back. You are now in intense pain; you can hardly even walk! Still, you must go to this job interview.

22. Your grandmother has prepared a meal for you — her famous Hungarian goulash. The last time you ate this stuff it made you so sick that you vomited. Your grandmother is in the next room, waiting for you to finish. You love your grandmother and you don't want to hurt her feelings, but you fear a reaction similar to your previous experience with her goulash.

23. You're in your office working on a report that you promised you would have ready for your boss by the end of the working day. It's close to quitting time, and you're far from finishing the report. You've already given him an excuse why you couldn't have the report completed last week, and you fear that if you don't hand him the report within the next hour, you will be fired.

24. You borrowed your friend's electric hedge clippers to do some gardening that you've been putting off. Your friend was reluctant to lend you the clippers because he just purchased them at considerable expense, but you convinced him that you would take good care of it. After taking a brief break, you try to restart the device, but it won't operate. It's broken! Your friend will be over to pick it up in a few minutes.

25. You've just hung up the phone after speaking with your daughter. She called to ask you to be careful not to dispose of the contents of a cup that's on your kitchen counter. She said that her engagement ring is inside the cup soaking in some jewelry cleaning solution. You look on the counter and discover that the cup is not there! You've already washed it out, but you don't recall seeing a ring inside the cup. You fear you may have dumped it down the drain.

26. You're a student taking a final examination in a classroom. If you don't pass this test, you will fail the course and your parents will be furious. Unfortunately, you're not doing very well on this test; you think you're well on your way to failing it. Sitting beside you is a very intelligent student who has unintentionally left his test paper exposed for you to see easily. You don't believe in cheating, but if you don't pass this test, your parents will make your life miserable.

27. You're sitting in a diner after finishing a delicious meal. In the past, you would have automatically lit a cigarette after such a meal, but your doctor has advised you to quit smoking. You haven't had a cigarette in a week. As you sit waiting for the check to arrive, some cigarette smoke from a neighboring table drifts over to your table, and you become very tempted to smoke. A cigarette machine is only a few steps away from you.

28. You've been fishing for hours, and you haven't caught a thing. Earlier, you bragged to all your friends about how great a fisherman you are. They're all waiting for you at the lodge. The sun has set; you can hardly see a thing, and you have to leave soon.

29. You are very angry with your son because yesterday was your birthday, and he hasn't sent a card or called. You really feel like calling him to tell him how angry you are, but you have your pride. Your phone is beside you.

30. A television program that you've been waiting to see for weeks is about to go on. Just as you settle down in your chair to watch the program, you remember that you're supposed to meet your friends downtown. You pop a tape into your VCR, only to discover that your VCR is broken.

31. You're sitting beside your telephone, trying to decide whether or not you should call this girl (or guy) whom you met last week. You know that you shouldn't hesitate to call because you really like this person, but you are extremely afraid of rejection. The last three women (or men) that you asked out on a date all turned you down.

32. You're in a log cabin with no electric or gas heat, only a fireplace. It's very cold and you'd like to start a fire, but you're out of firewood. If you don't get a fire going soon, you might freeze to death.

33. You're a vice president of a large company. You just hung up the phone after speaking with the company's president. He's directed you to fire one of your employees. What he doesn't know is that this employee is your best friend — a friend who helped you get the position that you now hold! You hear someone knocking on your office door. When you look through the window, you see that it's your friend.

34. It's the first chilly day of the fall season, and you've taken out a light jacket to wear to the store. When you try to button the jacket, you see that it's much too tight; you've gained some weight over the summer. Still, it's the only jacket you have, so you must wear it.

35. You're standing before your boyfriend's front door. You intend to go inside and tell him that you wish to break up with him; however, you don't have the courage to face him. You decide that the best thing to do is write a "Dear John" letter and leave it in his mailbox. As you begin to write, your pen runs out of ink. You don't have another one.

36. You're in your car on your way to work when your car runs out of gas. There isn't a gas station around for miles. Last week your boss told you that if you showed up late for work one more time, you would be fired.

37. Yesterday you met someone to whom you were very much attracted in an art gallery. To make a good impression on this person, you told her (or him) that you were an accomplished artist yourself, even though you never painted one brush stroke in your life. You've just hung up your phone after speaking with this person. She (or he) will be at your apartment in ten minutes to look at your paintings.

38. You're in your apartment trying to watch your favorite television program, but your neighbor in the adjoining apartment is blasting rock music on his stereo.

39. Your friend set you up on a blind date. You've seen a picture of this person; he (or she) is very attractive. It's only a few minutes before your date will arrive, and you're trying to figure out what to do with a huge pimple on the tip of your nose.

40. You have a horrible toothache; you've had it for a week now. It's become so bad that you can hardly chew even soft food without suffering excruciating pain. You've made an appointment to see your dentist tomorrow, but in the meantime, you're very hungry. You decide to try to eat something before you faint from hunger.

41. You're in your bedroom trying to get some sleep, but it's uncomfortably warm and your air conditioner is broken. You don't even own a fan.

42. You're a student about to stand in front of your class to give an oral report. As you rise from your seat, you notice a huge ink stain on your shirt from an uncapped felt-tip pen that you put in your pocket. You know that you will never hear the end of it if the class sees your shirt.

43. You're a student sitting at a table in your school's cafeteria doing some homework, a composition for your English class. It's a very important assignment that your teacher will collect in class next period, which begins in five minutes. Just as you finish the paper, you pick up a glass of soda to take a sip; but you accidentally spill the soda all over the paper, making it completely unreadable.

44. You're in the laundry room of your apartment building. You've just loaded all your laundry in three different washing machines. You've put coins in the machines and turned on the water when you realize that your box of laundry detergent is empty. It's late at night, no one else is around, and all the stores in the area are closed. Also, your laundry room has no detergent dispenser machine.

45. You've just spent an hour in a gym lifting weights. You haven't ever done this before, so you're in terrible pain. You can't move a muscle. You desperately need some aspirins, but, unfortunately, they're on the top shelf of your medicine cabinet. You can't lift your arms above your head to get them.

46. Foolishly, while painting the floor, you've painted yourself into the corner of a room. In the next room, the phone rings. You're expecting an important phone call.

47. You're a model at a fashion show trying to make a quick change; you're due on the runway in seconds. In your haste to get the outfit on quickly, you rip a sleeve right off the outfit!

48. You're an amateur astronomer about to photograph through your telescope a total solar eclipse, a once in a lifetime event that will only last a few minutes. As the time for the eclipse approaches, you try to remove the lens cap of the telescope, only to discover that it is stuck fast. You examine it closely and see that some shameless prankster has glued on your lens cap! You think it may take several minutes to scrape the glue off.

49. You're in your car driving to the airport to pick up your brother when one of your tires goes flat. You open the trunk of your car to take out your spare when you discover that you have no spare. There are no service stations around for miles, and your brother's plane lands in ten minutes.

50. You need to go food shopping; your refrigerator is nearly empty. Before you can go, however, you need to find your wallet. You seem to have misplaced it.

51. You're in an amusement park standing before a huge roller coaster. All your other friends have already gone on the ride. You'd like to join them, but you're deathly afraid of roller coasters.

52. It's Saturday morning, and you're scheduled to pitch today for your softball team's league championship game. You're the team's best pitcher; it is doubtful that the team can win without you. You know that your team is depending on you. However, you've woken up with chills and a fever, and you don't know if you can make it through an entire game.

53. You're in a used car dealership. You spot a car in your price range that would be perfect for you, except that it's green. You hate the color green. You swore that you would never buy a green car. You look around and see no other car in your price range.

54. You're in the woods hiking when you realize that you are completely lost. If you don't return to your campsite within the next few minutes, the rest of your party will be very concerned. Before you left, you were bragging about what a great woodsman you are.

55. The master of ceremonies at an awards banquet has just announced that you won the award of "Person of the Year." You had prepared a short speech of people to thank in case you won, but when you get to the podium, you go completely blank.

56. You're out hunting for buried treasure. You have a map that tells you exactly where the treasure is buried. You think you've found the spot, but before you can rejoice in your triumph, you realize that you forgot to bring a shovel! Other people looking for the treasure will undoubtedly arrive at the spot within a few moments.

57. You're walking to a friend's house when you stop at a fork in the road. This is the first time you've taken this particular route, so you're not sure which direction to take. Your friend is expecting you, and you're already late.

58. You're cooking on your stove top when some grease splatters and causes a small fire. You grab a small fire extinguisher, pull the pin, and aim it toward the fire, but when you squeeze the trigger, you discover that it is empty. In the meantime, the fire is beginning to spread.

59. You're a nightclub singer about to entertain a large crowd with a new song that you learned just yesterday. The band plays the introduction to the song, and when your cue comes to start singing, you forget the lyrics.

60. You're in your kitchen spreading the frosting on a cake that you've just baked. You're three-quarters of the way finished when you run out of frosting. You promised your little daughter that you'd have the cake ready for her birthday party, which begins in about fifteen minutes.

61. You're waiting to pick up your son from football practice. He was supposed to meet you in front of the field at five o'clock. It's now ten minutes past five and he's still not here. You have to get somewhere by 5:30, and if your son doesn't arrive soon, you will be late.

62. You've just been out jogging. You're very sweaty and in great need of a shower. When you get home and turn on the water, nothing happens. You call the water company and find out that a major water pipe broke somewhere down the street, and you won't have any water for a few hours.

63. You're a high school student trying to read a chapter from a textbook. You will be quizzed on this chapter tomorrow. However, it's very late, and you're struggling to stay awake.

64. You're sitting in a church or synagogue during a very solemn and quiet part of the service when you feel a sneezing fit about to come on. You know how embarrassed you will be if you begin to sneeze, so you do all you can to keep from sneezing.

65. You're sitting at a table in a restaurant trying to eavesdrop on a conversation that's taking place at the next table. Just as the conversation starts to get extremely interesting, the people talking lower their voices so that you can hardly make out a word they're saying. You are tempted to move closer to them, but you don't want to make it obvious that you're eavesdropping.

66. You're a thief looking through the closets and drawers in the bedroom of a home that you intend to rob. As you begin to load your bag with some valuables that you've found, you hear the homeowners arrive. They settle down in their living room to watch some television. You try to escape through the bedroom window, but it's locked and you can't open it. The only exit to the house is out the door and through the living room.

67. You've just come home from the dentist. The shot of anesthetic that the dentist gave you hasn't worn off yet, making it nearly impossible for you to speak clearly. The phone rings, and you remember that your boss said that he'd call around this time to ask you some very important questions about a project that you've been working on. You promised him that you'd be home to answer his questions.

68. Your father is a police officer, and you found a pair of his handcuffs. You start playing with them and accidentally handcuff yourself to the leg of a table. Your father will be home at any moment, and if he sees that you've been playing with the handcuffs, you will be in a great deal of trouble.

69. You're a concert pianist about to perform before a large crowd. When you start to play, you hear that the piano is painfully out of tune. The people in the audience have paid good money to hear you play, but you don't want to tarnish your image by playing an out-of-tune piano.

70. You hurt your ankle last night, but you didn't realize just how badly you hurt it until you woke up in pain this morning. Your ankle is swollen, and you can hardly walk. You have to report to your job as a letter carrier for the U.S. Postal Service in an hour. The job, of course, requires lots of walking. You've already taken all of your sick leave days this year, and you fear that if you don't show up for work today, you will be fired.

71. You're in a public beach house, and you have to go to the bathroom badly. When you walk inside the bathroom, you see a series of pay toilets — and *only* pay toilets. Unfortunately, you have no money at all!

72. You've been invited to a party. When you arrive, you notice that people walking into the party are dressed in costumes. You check your invitation and you see that it is, indeed, an masquerade party — a fact that you did not realize until this moment. You can't go back home because the taxi that dropped you off is already gone.

73. You're placing a letter in a U.S. Postal Service mailbox. As you drop the letter into the mailbox, the clasp of your watch suddenly becomes unhooked, and your watch falls into the mailbox. The watch was given to you by your dearly departed grandfather; to you, it is priceless. You know that it's a federal offense to tamper with a U.S. Postal Service mailbox, but you must get that watch!

74. You're browsing in a china shop. You pick up a handcrafted plate priced at $100, and while you're examining it, you accidentally drop it and it shatters. You'd hate to have to pay for this plate, especially since you only have thirteen dollars on you. You're not sure if the store manager saw you drop the plate.

75. If you don't make a phone call right away, a once in a lifetime opportunity will pass you by. The only phone around is a pay phone. Unfortunately, you have no change, nor do you have a phone company credit card.

76. Yesterday you hurt your ankle, and your doctor suggested that you stay off it for a while. You're a star player on your soccer team; the entire team is depending on you to play in today's championship game. If you play, you may cause irreparable damage to your ankle. You're in your room trying to decide whether or not you should get dressed for the game.

77. You have to sign some important documents, but you're right-handed and your right hand is in a cast.

78. You're in an open area of a park trying to fly a kite, but the wind has died down. Your brother will be meeting you shortly with his five-year-old son, and you promised the child that you'd have the kite flying high by the time he arrives.

79. You just bought a new VCR, and after you opened the box, you noticed that the operating instructions are written only in Japanese. You've called the appliance store where you bought the VCR, and you were told that instructions are not available in English. Also, the item is nonreturnable.

80. You need to catch a plane that is scheduled to take off in ten minutes. You're in your car stuck in a traffic jam about a mile from the airport.

81. In ten minutes your dinner guests will arrive. Everything appears to be ready, but when you open the oven door to take out the roast, you see that it is completely raw. You forgot to turn on the oven!

82. You just spent a week at your friend's apartment taking care of his pets while he was away on vacation. You were very conscientious about feeding and walking his dog, but moments before he is due to return, you realize that you forgot to feed his expensive tropical fish. You check the fish tank and see that they are all dead!

83. Last night ten inches of snow fell, and you need to clear the snow from your driveway so that you can get to your car and drive to work. Your boss doesn't have much sympathy for people who use the weather and road conditions as an excuse for coming to work late. As you pull the cord to start your gas-powered snow blower, you notice that it is out of gas. You don't own a hand shovel.

84. You're moving very slowly these days because last week you twisted your ankle and you're still limping. You're going to make an attempt to cross a very busy street.

85. Your date will be picking you up at any moment, and you're running a bit late. Your hair is soaking wet because you've just washed it. You turn on your hair dryer to blow dry your hair and nothing happens. It's broken.

86. Your head is pounding; you have an awful headache. You open your medicine cabinet and take out an aspirin bottle. You open it and see that it's empty. You must find a way to get rid of this terrible headache!

87. You borrowed your friend's brand-new BMW convertible to go to a shopping mall. When you return to the car after shopping, you notice a huge dent on the left front fender. Your friend is the type of person who becomes very upset when he notices even a tiny scratch on the car. You promised to have the car back to him in perfect condition by this afternoon.

88. You've been playing the same six numbers in the weekly state lottery for the past few years. Every week you buy a lottery ticket. When you check today's newspaper to see if your numbers have come up, you become ecstatic when you see that they finally have! Frantically, you search for your ticket, but you seem to have misplaced it. You need that ticket to claim your $25,000 cash prize!

89. You don't want to admit that you've gained weight. You can prove to yourself that you are still your same slim self by putting on an old pair of jeans. You're determined to fit into those jeans, but pulling up the zipper seems to be quite challenging for you at the moment.

90. You're a teacher who is about to grade your class's final examinations. This exam counts for half of the students' final course grade. You open up a folder to take out the exams, but you see that the folder contains nothing but scrap paper. Suddenly you realize that you threw out the folder containing the exams, thinking that it was the one with the scrap paper!

91. You're at your only daughter's high school graduation ceremony. In a few minutes, the school principal will be handing your daughter her diploma. You pick up your camera to make sure that it's working properly when you realize that you forgot to load it with film!

92.   You're vacationing in the Bahamas, anxious to fly home to New York City because your father called a little while ago to tell you that your mother has become very ill. When you get to the airport, you're told that all flights to New York City have been delayed because of a snow storm that has closed down all New York airports. No one is sure when they will reopen.

93.   You promised your spouse that you'd set your new VCR to tape a program that airs today when you both will be at work. Minutes before you leave to go to work, you try to set the VCR, but you can't figure out how it works. Your spouse has already left, and you can't find the VCR's instruction booklet.

94.   You're conducting an orchestra. Moments before you have to cue the string section to begin playing, your music stand falls apart and the score scatters all over the floor. You'd normally give them the cue from memory, but this is a piece that you're not very familiar with. You desperately need the score in front of you!

95.   You're leaving work at six o'clock at night, an hour after everyone else has already quit for the day. You put the key that opens your car door into the keyhole, and the key breaks in the door. You can't open the door! No one else is around. You can't even go back into the building where you work to make a phone call because the building has already been locked up tight.

96.   You just brought home a large box containing the pieces to a bookcase that you bought. After laying the pieces out all over the floor, you look in your tool box for a screwdriver. Unfortunately, you can't find one. You need a screwdriver to assemble the bookcase.

97.   You walk into a crowded elevator with a cup of hot coffee in each hand. As you stand shoulder to shoulder with the other people on the elevator, you feel that you are about to sneeze. You'd like to put down the coffee and cover your mouth with your handkerchief, but you don't have enough time or room to do that.

98. It's early in the morning. Everyone else in your family is still sleeping but will be awakening at any moment. Last night you promised your family that you would make bacon and eggs for everyone, but when you look in the refrigerator, you see that there are no eggs. You would run to a grocery store to buy some, but none is open yet.

99. Your house is for sale. Your real estate broker just called to tell you that she will be over in fifteen minutes with some people who would like to look at the house. Unfortunately, the house is a mess; you haven't had time to clean up after a party that you had last night. You're very anxious to sell this house; you haven't had anyone look at it in quite a while, and you fear that they won't be interested in the house because of the mess.

100. You're an actor waiting for a rehearsal to begin. As you wait, you look at your rehearsal schedule and notice that you are supposed to have your lines memorized by today's rehearsal. You still haven't memorized all your lines. Your director is a dictator, and you know that he will be furious with you when he learns that you haven't memorized your lines.

4

Using Physical Positions

We use more than verbal language to communicate our thoughts and feelings; we also use body language. The way we sit, stand, and move all help reveal attitudes and emotions that we frequently can't conceal. The hidden truth about people is often given away by their body language. How many times have you been able to assess someone's personality accurately even before the person has had a chance to say one word? On the other hand, people who are keenly aware of the power of nonverbal communication can use this knowledge to their advantage.

Good actors spend their lives studying the powerful effects of body language. They realize that in the theater, the visual carries as much importance as the verbal, sometimes more. Perhaps the most significant scene of William Gibson's *The Miracle Worker* occurs when Annie Sullivan physically struggles with Helen for a period of about five minutes. It's in this key scene of the play where Annie makes her first substantial breakthrough with Helen, and the audience learns much about Annie Sullivan's determination and Helen Keller's obstinacy — and it's all done without any dialogue at all!

The improvisation starters in this chapter use the nonverbal elements of communication to begin the action. All character relationships and conflicts are determined by the players themselves, solely by the way they are positioned. As you run these improvisations with your players, you may be surprised at the direction in which they will turn. That's part of the fun. In real life, the nonverbal messages that we send are interpreted differently by different people. Often when we think we're communicating a particular thought or feeling, we're actually communicating something completely different. You will see this principle demonstrated in many of the following improvisations.

These improvisations are very easy to run. Have your players take the stage or playing area and ask them to stand facing full front to the audience, feet together and arms at their sides. Now read aloud one of the descriptions of the physical positions provided below. When you are satisfied that your players are "frozen" in the correct positions, give the signal to begin by snapping your fingers, or by saying "go" or "unfreeze" or something similar. If the improvisation involves more than one person, the first player to speak determines the direction the improvisation will take. Take, for example, a two-player improvisation in which Player One is positioned with his or her hands in the air, and Player Two is pointing at Player One. If Player One speaks first by saying, "Please don't shoot," then Player Two must follow immediately with a logical response. However, if Player Two should speak first by saying, "That's enough exercise for today," then Player One must go along with that. Another way to run these improvisations is to decide beforehand who will speak first.

One important rule: Anything the players first say or do must be prompted by their physical positions and, in the case of two players, their physical relationship to each other. If, in your judgment, this doesn't happen, stop the improvisation and have the players begin again.

Encourage your players to be creative. A player who is asked to extend an index finger into the air may be inspired to exclaim, "We're Number One!" while pretending to be a football player. A more creative player might shout, "Hey! See if you can toss that ring around my finger!" Clichéd responses should be avoided as much as possible.

You may use the following guide questions when discussing the performances with your players and audience:

1. How did the players' physical positions lead them to speak or behave the way they did?

2. Did the players' physical positions help determine their actions and objectives?

3. Did the players' physical positions serve as obstacles for themselves or the other person in the scene?

4. Did the players use a creative approach, or were you able to predict more or less what they said and did?

5. Did the players initially say or do anything that wasn't suggested by their physical positions?

6. Did the players maintain a posture that was similar to their opening position, or did they completely divert from their original positions?

7. Did the players' attitudes, moods, or emotions change throughout the performance?

ONE PLAYER

Begin by instructing the player to stand center stage, facing full front with feet together and arms to the sides. From there, have the player move into one of the physical positions described below. (Note: Unless specifically instructed to face left or right, the player should remain facing full front.)

1. Keep your arms at your sides, and look directly above you.

2. Place your hands on your hips, face left, and look down.

3. Stand on one foot.

4. Face left, and point toward the left with your left hand.

5. Put your right hand on top of your head, and your left hand on your left hip.

6. Fold your arms and fix your eyes toward the right.

7. Stand on a chair, and extend your right hand above you.

8. Extend both arms above you, and open your hands.

9. Raise only your right hand high into the air.

10. Place both hands on your stomach.

11. Place your right hand on your left elbow, and face right.

12. Clasp your hands together above your head, tilt your head upward, and close your eyes.

13. Touch your left shoulder with your left hand, and touch your right shoulder with your right hand.

14. Hold your chin with your right hand.

15. Extend your right arm, and open your hand with your palm facing up.

16. Touch your nose with the index finger of your right hand, extend your left arm to your left, and open your left hand with your palm facing left.

17. Place your left knee on the ground, and put your hands on your hips.

18. Kneel with both knees on the ground and look above you.

19. Fold your arms and open your eyes as wide as you can.

20. Extend your right hand into the air and make a fist.

21. Sit in a chair with your legs crossed and your arms folded.

22. Sit in a chair, and cover your eyes with your hands.

23. Sit in a chair, and place your hands over your ears.

24. Sit in a chair, extend your left arm to your left, make a fist with your left hand, and place your right hand on your right knee.

25. Sit in a chair, extend both arms directly in front of you, and open your hands with your palms facing the audience.

26. Sit on the floor with your legs crossed, and fold your arms.

27. Sit on the floor with your legs extended and your ankles crossed, lean back, and support yourself with your hands on the floor behind you.

28. Kneel on both knees, and place both hands on the floor in front of you.

29. Kneel on your right knee only, extend your right arm straight out to your right, and turn your head only to the right. Place your left hand on your left hip.

30. Extend your right arm straight out to your right, make a ninety degree angle with your right elbow, and open your right hand so that your palm faces the audience.

31. Tilt your head down, and place your right hand on your forehead.

32. Extend your right arm straight out in front of you, and hold your right elbow with your left hand.

33. Extend both arms straight out to either side, bend your elbows to form ninety degree angles, and point straight up with the index finger of each hand.

34. Sit in a chair, fold your arms across your stomach, and bend over slightly.

35. Spread your feet apart about two feet, bend your waist toward your right side, and place your left hand on top of your head. Let your right arm hang.

36. Without moving your shoulders, point to the left with your right hand, and point to the right with your left hand. Your arms will be crossed. Look straight ahead.

37. Kneel on your right knee only, and place both hands on the ground before you.

38. Raise your right hand, and make a circle with your thumb and index finger.

39. Make an "X" with the index fingers of your left and right hands, holding them a few inches in front of your nose.

40. Place both hands behind your back.

41. Place your right hand behind your back, and extend your left hand toward the audience. Open your hand so that your palm faces up.

42. Place your right hand behind your back, and hold your right shoulder with your left hand.

43. Sit on the edge of a chair with your knees and feet together, and place your right hand under your right knee, and your left hand under your left knee.

44. Cover your right eye with your right hand.

45. Tilt your head down, make a fist with your left hand, and place it on your forehead.

46. Cover your mouth with both hands. Open your eyes as wide as possible.

47. Place your right hand behind your head.

48. Place both hands behind your head.

49. Bend over and touch your toes. (You may bend your knees if you have to!)

50. Tilt your head to the right, and cup your right hand around your right ear.

TWO PLAYERS

Begin by instructing Player One to stand at stage right, facing full front with feet together and arms to the sides. Instruct Player Two to take the same position, except at stage left. The players should stand only a few feet away from each other. From there, have your players move into one of the physical positions described below. (Note: Unless specifically instructed to face left or right, the players should remain facing full front.)

1. **Player One:** Fold your arms, and face right.

   Player Two: Place both hands over your ears, and close your eyes.

2. **Player One:** Sit on the floor with your legs crossed and arms folded.

   Player Two: Turn facing Player One, and point at him with your right hand.

3. **Player One:** Extend both hands high into the air, and look to your right.

   Player Two: Face right, kneel on both knees, and extend both hands high into the air.

4. **Player One:** Face left, clasp both of your hands together (interlocking your fingers), extend your arms before you, and kneel on your right knee.

   Player Two: Face left, and fold your arms.

5. **Player One:** Face left, extend your right hand toward Player Two, and look directly above you.

   Player Two: Face right, grasp Player One's right hand with your right hand, and look directly above you.

6. **Player One:** Face right, and fold your arms.

   Player Two: Face right, and place your right hand on Player One's right shoulder.

7. **Player One:** Tilt your head down, and cover your eyes with your hands.

Player Two: Stand at Player One's left side, and place your right hand on Player One's right shoulder (from behind).

8. **Player One:** Kneel on both knees, and extend both arms straight ahead, pointing with the index finger of each hand.

Player Two: Take the same position as Player One.

9. **Player One:** Bend slightly at the waist, and place both hands on your stomach.

Player Two: Face right, bend slightly at the waist, look at Player One's stomach, and point to it with your right index finger.

10. **Player One:** Sit on the floor, knees together and legs bent, lean back a bit, and support yourself by placing your hands on the floor behind you.

Player Two: Face left, and raise both hands high into the air.

11. **Player One:** While keeping the ball of your left foot where it is, take one step forward with your right foot, make a fist with your right hand, and raise it high into the air.

Player Two: Take the same position as Player One.

12. **Player One:** Extend your left arm straight out to your left, and your right arm straight out to your right. Bend both elbows ninety degrees so that your hands are up. Open your hands, and spread your fingers wide apart.

Player Two: Face right, look at Player One, and fold your arms.

13. **Player One:** Place your right hand on your left shoulder, and turn only your head to the left.

Player Two: Make two fists, and raise both arms into the air.

14. **Player One:** Bend slightly at the waist, place your hands on your knees, and look straight ahead.

Player Two: Kneel on your right knee, and point straight ahead using your right index finger.

15. **Player One:** Raise both hands, palms facing each other, with your arms at about a forty-five degree angle to your shoulders. Don't bend your elbows. Look above you.

Player Two: Fold your arms, and turn only your head to the left.

16. **Player One:** Bend your elbows so that your arms form ninety degree angles. Open your hands, palms facing each other. Now move your hands toward each other until they are only a few inches apart. Focus your eyes on the space between your hands.

Player Two: Do the same thing as Player One, except move your hands away from each other until they are about three feet apart.

17. **Player One:** Sit in a chair, and fold your arms. Keep your feet and knees together.

Player Two: Sit in a chair, extend your legs forward, and cross your ankles. Sink down in your chair a little bit, and place your hands behind your head.

18. **Player One:** Sit on the edge of a chair, bend your waist forward, move your knees and feet apart slightly, and place your left elbow on your left knee fixing your elbow at a ninety degree angle. Make a fist with your left hand, and place your right hand on your right knee. Look straight ahead.

Player Two: Stand directly behind Player One, and place your hands on his shoulders. Look straight ahead.

19. **Player One:** Fold your arms, and face right. Look over your left shoulder toward Player Two.

Player Two: Fold your arms, and face left. Look over your right shoulder toward Player One.

20. **Player One:** Face left, raise your right hand, extend it forward a bit, and open your palm so that it faces Player Two.

Player Two: Face right, and place your open right palm against Player One's open right palm.

21. **Player One:** Open your right palm, make a ninety degree angle with your right elbow, and move your hand so that your palm is up. Now make a fist with your left hand, and rest it on your open right palm, left thumb on top. Look at your hands.

Player Two: Face right, and place your right hand on Player One's left shoulder.

22. **Player One:** Extend your right arm straight out to your right. Make a fist with your right hand, and point your thumb up. Turn your head only to the right.

Player Two: Extend your left arm straight out to your left. Make a fist with your left hand, and point your thumb up. Turn your head only to the left.

23. **Player One:** Raise your right hand into the air, and form a "V" with your middle and index fingers.

Player Two: Extend your right arm straight ahead, make a fist with your right hand, and point your thumb down.

24. **Player One:** Place your open right palm against your open left palm, place the fingers of each hand against each other, and cross your thumbs. Position your hands so that they are a few inches away from your stomach. Kneel on both knees. Tilt your head up, and look above you.

Player Two: Stand behind Player One, and place your right hand on Player One's right shoulder.

25. **Player One:** While keeping your left foot where it is, slide your right foot a little toward your right. Hold your chin with your right hand, and place your left hand on your left hip.

Player Two: Face right, and extend both hands before you, palms up.

26. **Player One:** Face left, extend your right hand toward Player Two, and open your palm so that it faces him.

Player Two: Face right, and extend both hands into the air, palms open.

27. **Player One:** Face right, and cover your mouth with both hands.

    Player Two: Face left, and fold your arms.

28. **Player One:** Face left, and point at Player Two.

    Player Two: Face right, and point at Player One.

29. **Player One:** Place the tip of your right index finger against the right side of your head.

    Player Two: Take the same position as Player One.

30. **Player One:** Face left, and extend your right hand toward Player Two, palm up.

    Player Two: Face right, and place your right palm face down on Player One's right palm.

31. **Player One:** Extend both arms before you, and open your hands, palms up. Look above you.

    Player Two: Raise your right fist into the air, and look up.

32. **Player One:** Face right, extend your right arm before you, and open your right hand, palm facing the audience. Extend your left arm behind you, and open your hand, palm facing away from the audience. Keep the ball of your left foot where it is, and take one step with your right foot.

    Player Two: Take the same position as Player One.

33. **Player One:** Put your index fingers in both ears.

    Player Two: Extend both arms high into the air. Keep your hands open.

34. **Player One:** Face right, and place the back of your right hand across your eyes.

    Player Two: Face left, and place the back of your left hand against your eyes.

35. **Player One:** Extend both arms out to your left and right, bend your elbows ninety degrees, and cross the middle and index fingers of each hand.

    Player Two: Put your index fingers in each ear.

36. **Player One:** Tilt your head to the left.

Player Two: Stand with your right arm against Player One's left arm, and tilt your head to the right.

37. **Player One:** Place your hands on your lower back, and bend forward slightly.

Player Two: Face right, and hold Player One's left upper arm with your right hand.

38. **Player One:** Face left, extend your right arm toward Player Two, and make a fist with your right hand. Position your hand so that your thumb is on top.

Player Two: Face right, make a fist with your right hand, and place it on top of Player One's fist with the pinky side of your fist resting on Player One's thumb.

39. **Player One:** Face left, and raise both your hands high into the air.

Player Two: Face right, extend your right arm toward Player One, and open your right hand, palm facing Player One.

40. **Player One:** Face left, get on your hands and knees, and look at the floor just ahead of you.

Player Two: Face right, get on your hands and knees, and look at the floor just ahead of you.

41. **Player One:** Sit in a chair, place your hands on your lap, and turn your head toward the right.

Player Two: Sit in a chair, place your hands on your lap, and turn your head toward the left.

42. **Player One:** Sit in a chair, and place your right hand over your mouth. Turn your head toward the right.

Player Two: Face right, make two fists, and place them on your hips.

43. **Player One:** Place your right hand against the right side of your face.

   Player Two: Place your left hand on your stomach, and bend forward slightly.

44. **Player One:** Place your right hand on top of your head, and place the back of your left palm under your chin.

   Player Two: Face Player One, and cover your mouth with your right hand.

45. **Player One:** Face left, and place your right hand over your mouth. Look at Player Two.

   Player Two: Kneel on both knees, and place your right hand on your left shoulder.

46. **Player One:** Sit in a chair, place your right hand on top of your head, and place your left hand on your left knee.

   Player Two: Take the same position as Player One.

47. **Player One:** Face left, place your left hand over your mouth, and point at Player Two.

   Player Two: Face left, and fold your arms.

48. **Player One:** Face left, and place your hands over your ears.

   Player Two: Face right, and point at Player One with your right hand.

49. **Player One:** Tilt your head down, and place your hands behind your neck.

   Player Two: Stand beside Player One, and place your right hand on Player One's left shoulder.

50. **Player One:** Place your right hand behind your back.

   Player Two: Stand behind Player One, and hold his right wrist with your right hand.

5

Using Lines of Dialogue

Many beginning actors don't know how to listen — on stage, that is. They receive their scripts, memorize their lines, and try to perfect the exact way each line will be delivered. Once they decide which specific vocal inflections and facial expressions work best, they make sure that each line comes across exactly the same way for every single performance. After a while, it no longer becomes necessary to listen to the other actors on stage. As long as they recognize their cues, they're safe. Why bother worrying about an honest response to another character on stage when you've already figured out the perfect way to deliver your lines?

Obviously, real life doesn't work this way. We respond to more than just words; we respond to the *way* words are spoken. If someone were to call you an idiot, you might become very angry, or you might laugh — it all depends on your perception of the person's tone of voice and physical expression.

Theater, of course, is a reflection of real life. If the audience of a play were to sense that the characters weren't really listening to each other, they might not be so willing to *suspend their disbelief* that they're watching a real-life situation, as English poet and critic Samuel Taylor Coleridge suggested all members of the audience do when they watch a play.

One of the reasons acting instructors use improvisations is to teach the actor to listen. Since no words or actions have been prepared ahead of time, the actor *must* listen in order to respond. The improvisation starters in this chapter force the player to listen very carefully to how the other player in the scene delivers his first line, since that line will determine the direction that the entire improvisation will take. He will be compelled to respond not only to the *words* that he hears, but also to the meaning *beneath* those words.

To run these improvisations, have two players take the stage and whisper one of the following lines to *one* of the players. *The other player must not know the line in advance.* Once the player delivers the line, the other player should respond appropriately, and the improvisation should continue until a signal is given to stop.

Note: The player with the first line of dialogue doesn't necessarily have to begin speaking immediately. Some silent action may precede the line. For example, if the line is, "What's been going on here?", the player might look around at the condition of the room for a while before speaking. However, the other actor must not say anything until the line is spoken.

You may use the following guide questions when discussing the performances with your players and audience:

1. How would you describe the first player's tone of voice, attitude, emotional state, or mood when he spoke the first line?

2. Were you surprised by the second player's response to the first line? Why or why not? Would you have responded in a similar way?

3. Did the first line spoken serve to help the players determine their actions and objectives?

4. What kinds of obstacles faced each player? Did the obstacles directly result from the first line spoken?

5. Do you think that the first player delivered the first line in the most conventional way? How could the line have been delivered differently to evoke a completely different response from the second player?

6. Describe the overall mood of the scene.

1. I like it here.

2. I don't know what I'm doing here.

3. I need help.

4. I have to talk to you.

5. I'm sorry.

6. I'm here.

7. I'm exhausted.

8. I'm starving.

9. I've solved the problem.

10. I've never seen anything like it!

11. Let's get going.

12. Let's try to get to the bottom of this.

13. Let's put our cards on the table.

14. Let's not fight anymore.

15. Let's try to start over.

16. Let's pretend that yesterday never happened.

17. Let's try to have a good time.

18. Let's do something fun today.

19. Let's face the facts.

20. Let's get out while we can.

21. You shouldn't have come here.

22. You have blood on your shirt.

23. You don't know what I've been through today.

24. You have some nerve.

25. You didn't listen to a word I said yesterday.

26. You have the wrong idea.

27. You must have something to say about this.

28. You're in a lot of trouble.

29. You're never going to believe what just happened.

30. You're the last person I thought I'd run into here.

31. We need to talk.

32. We were fired.

33. We only have a few seconds.

34. We need help.

35. We're going to be fired.

36. We're through.

37. We're not supposed to be here.

38. We're going to like this.

39. We're not going to make it.

40. We're never going to get out of here alive.

41. Don't look at me like that.

42. Don't get me started.

43. Don't try to fool me.

44. Don't pretend that I'm not here.

45. Don't do that.

46. Don't make me laugh.

47. Don't leave here until you're finished.

48. Don't pay any attention to that.

49. Don't cry.

50. Don't underestimate yourself.

51. This is it.

52. This is good.

53. This is bad.

54. This is ridiculous.

55. This must be the place.

56. This needs work.

57. This will never work.

58. This looks like the answer.

59. This doesn't make sense.

60. This is going to be a problem.

61. Who are you?

62. Who do you think you are?

63. Who died and made you boss?

64. Who gave you permission to be here?

65. Who should I make this out to?

66. Who needs me here?

67. Who do think you're kidding?

68. Who sent you here?

69. Who let you in?

70. Who made this mess?

71. What is your name?

72. What made you come back here?

73. What is your problem?

74. What can I do for you?

75. What do you want?

76. What kind of fool do you think I am?

77. What are you going to do to me?

78. What is this?

79. What will it take to be rid of you?

80. What am I going to do with you?

81. Where did you come from?

82. Where do you think you're going?

83. Where will this all end?

84. Where in the world have you been?

85. Where can I go to avoid running into you?

86. Where is the money?

87. Where is my wife (or husband)?

88. Where did he go?

89. Where can I catch the bus?

90. Why are you here?

91. Why don't you get lost?

92. Why can't we be friends?

93. Why did I know you'd be here?

94. Why won't you forgive me?

95. Why don't you come with me?

96. Why do I come running back to you all the time?

97. Why do bad things always happen to me?

98. Why was I fired?

99. Why didn't you call me last night?

100. Why do I always have to come looking for you?

101. Are you all right?

102. Are we ever going to speak to each other again?

103. Are all men (or women) like you?

104. Are you ever going to leave?

105. Are you in the right place?

106. Are you serious?

107. Are my eyes deceiving me?

108. Are you here for good?

109. Are your parents home?

110. Are my friends here yet?

111. Is that really you?

112. Is this the right place?

113. Is your name Sam?

114. Is that all there is?

115. Is this mine or yours?

116. Is my tie on straight?

117. Is this your way of saying you're sorry?

118. Isn't this a coincidence?

119. Isn't there a place I can go to be alone?

120. Isn't what happened to him a shame?

121. How do you do?

122. How did you get in here?

123. How can you ever forgive me?

124. How can I make this up to you?

125. How did you do that?

126. How can we settle this?

127. How can I help you?

128. How is your mother?

129. How can I make you believe me?

130. How was your day?

131. Do you belong here?

132. Do we know each other?

133. Do you always show up where you're not wanted?

134. Do you mind?

135. Does it have to end this way?

136. Does this make sense to you?

137. Don't you have any self-respect?

138. Don't you want to get going?

139. Didn't I make myself clear yesterday?

140. Didn't I see you here yesterday?

141. When did you get here?

142. When are you leaving?

143. When will you ever learn?

144. When will this all end?

145. When does the show start?

146. When will you forget me?

147. When will you stop bothering me?

148. When can I see you?

149. When can I come back?

150. When will it be safe?

151. Have you seen my glasses?

152. Have we been here before?

153. Have I done something wrong?

154. Have you been good?

155. Have we seen the last of him?

156. Have I got two heads or something?

157. Have you had enough?

158. Have we met before?

159. Have I been sleeping all this time?

160. Have you done all your work?

161. I guess it's my lucky day.

162. You will never believe what just happened.

163. He won't confess.

164. She doesn't want to talk to you.

165. I don't need this.

166. You can't be serious.

167. He means business.

168. She's not as bad as you think she is.

169. We can only stay for a few minutes.

170. They let us down.

171. I'm going to call the police.

172. You don't know what I've been going through.

173. He said to wait here for him.

174. She left about an hour ago.

175. We might as well give up.

176. They don't have a clue.

177. I want you out of here, now!

178. You don't have to stay if you don't want to.

179. He likes to think he owns the place.

180. She doesn't deserve to be treated that way.

181. We have to do something about this.

182. They left without saying good-bye.

183. I'm not done yet.

184. You must realize that your situation is hopeless.

185. He doesn't know you're here.

186. She wasted enough of our time.

187. We can't let this discourage us.

188. They don't know what they're getting into.

189. I'm waiting for an apology.

190. You don't owe me a thing.

191. He warned me not to come here.

192. She wanted me to tell you that she's okay.

193. We must not let them get to us.

194. They probably forgot we were here.

195. I've waited here long enough.

196. You may not want to hear this, but it's over.

197. He won't be back, so don't worry about it.

198. She said to stop it now.

199. We have to be quiet.

200. They said to come back later.

6

Using the Environment

Picture yourself standing in the middle of a crowded amusement park. Imagine the sights, the smells, the sounds, your feeling of exhilaration as you decide whether to take another ride on the roller coaster or meet your friends at the video arcade. Now imagine yourself sitting in a quiet library, so quiet that you can hear yourself breathe. Around you, others are deep in concentration or browsing through huge stacks of books. Suddenly, you break the silence with a loud sneeze and become embarrassed by the stares from those surrounding you.

Obviously, our surroundings greatly affect the way we feel and behave. However, many beginning actors don't use their surroundings properly. Have you ever seen a play in which an actor is supposed to be walking into a room for the first time in his life, yet it appears by his expression that he's been there many times before? A skilled actor knows the importance of considering the environment while preparing for a role.

Listed below are one hundred acting environments. Direct any number of players to take the stage or playing area, and then announce the setting. As soon as you give the signal to begin, the players are free to say and do anything they like, as long as their words and actions make sense within the environment that surrounds them.

You may use the following guide questions when discussing the performances with your players and audience:

1. How did the players use the environment to develop the improvisation? Did it play a significant role in determining their actions and objectives?

2. What conflicts developed as a direct result of the environment?

3. Did the environment prove to be an obstacle to any or all of the players in the scene?

4. What did the players see, hear, touch, taste, or smell in the environment? Which sense played the most significant role in the improvisation?

5. Do you think you would have behaved the same way in this environment? If not, what would you have done differently?

1. A roadside diner at dinner time.

2. An 80,000 person capacity football stadium seconds before a game is about to begin.

3. An abandoned railroad station in a ghost town.

4. A high school classroom during homeroom period at eight o'clock in the morning.

5. A street in a large city during rush hour.

6. The rooftop of a thirty-story building on a dark night.

7. A secluded area of a large park.

8. A prison cell in a small town jail.

9. A cemetery on a clear, moonlit night.

10. A major airport at ten o'clock in the morning.

11. A six-foot trench in a battlefield during the height of a battle.

12. A small rowboat in the middle of an enormous lake.

13. An immense ocean liner in the middle of the Atlantic Ocean.

14. The cockpit of a large jet airliner 30,000 feet in the air.

15. Inside a tank during a battle.

16. The rest room of an elegant restaurant.

17. A busy gambling casino in Las Vegas.

18. A large city police station.

19. The first hole of a golf course at six o'clock in the morning.

20. A kindergarten classroom at lunchtime.

21. The cafeteria of a large high school during the last lunch period of the day.

22. A modern art museum.

23. The newsroom of a local television station.

24. A bench in the middle of a gigantic shopping mall.

25. An outdoor basketball court.

26. The kitchen of a busy restaurant.

27. A scientist's research laboratory.

28. An old-fashioned candy store.

29. The emergency room of a hospital.

30. A dark and secluded cave.

31. The middle of a thick forest.

32. An archaeologist's excavation site.

33. An ocean beach at sunrise.

34. The backstage area of a theater.

35. The waiting room of a doctor's office.

36. A children's playground.

37. A room in a college dormitory.

38. The vestibule of a church on a Sunday morning.

39. A greenhouse filled with flowers.

40. An empty gymnasium.

41. A rose garden.

42. The basement of an abandoned building.

43. An empty in-ground swimming pool.

44. A bank building.

45. An elegant clothing store.

46. A prison yard late at night.

47. A room with padded walls.

48. The locker room of a gym.

49. A large walk-in refrigerator.

50. An underground tunnel.

51. A submarine.

52. The summit of a mountain 10,000 feet in the air.

53. The cab of an eighteen-wheel tractor trailer.

54. A cornfield of a farm.

55. A barnyard filled with animals.

56. A mechanic's garage.

57. A new car dealer showroom.

58. A snow-covered field.

59. A morgue.

60. A fishing boat out at sea.

61. A large zoo.

62. A tropical jungle.

63. A dude ranch.

64. A musician's rehearsal studio.

65. A boardwalk near an ocean shore.

66. A poorly lit alleyway between two tall buildings on a dark night.

67. A junkyard filled with scrap metal.

68. The edge of a thirty-foot cliff hanging over the sea.

69. A flooded basement of a house.

70. A taxi in a big city.

71. An aircraft carrier out at sea.

72. A helicopter.

73. A garbage dump.

74. A fishing pier.

75. The front porch of a house.

76. A general store in a small New England town.

77. The midway of a crowded carnival.

78. The dance floor of a crowded nightclub.

79. The computer room of a major corporation.

80. A steamboat on a river.

81. A boxing ring.

82. A space shuttle in orbit.

83. A road construction site.

84. A movie theater.

85. A concert hall.

86. A furniture store.

87. A portrait artist's studio.

88. A carpenter's workshop.

89. An open area in a desert.

90. The fire escape of an apartment building.

91. An underground bomb shelter.

92. A deserted island beach.

93. A funeral parlor at night.

94. A large parking lot.

95. A courtroom.

96. A wax museum.

97. An elegant hotel room.

98. A hospital room.

99. A crowded commuter train.

100. A horse racing track.

7

Using Props

If you're in a familiar place right now, take a minute to stop and look around you. You probably see many things that you've seen a thousand times before. Perhaps some of those things belong to you, or maybe they belong to people you know. Most likely, many of those things bring to mind particular memories of places you've been or people you know. Some of those things might even elicit an emotional response from you.

Props can provide interesting and creative ways to start improvisations. Just as the objects surrounding you can bring to mind particular thoughts, an actor with a vivid imagination can think of many ways to use props that he or she has never seen before. Let's say you're given a pencil and then asked to improvise a scene using it as an important part of the improvisation. You're given no other setting, actions, objectives, or hint of a situation. What might you do with the pencil? Your most obvious choice is to write with it. You might write a letter or a grocery list. If you're a bit more creative, you might draw a picture. If you're very creative, you might use the pencil for something other than writing or drawing. You might pry open a lid, or maybe punch holes in the top of a shoe box. You're only limited by your imagination. Improvising with props is one way to exercise the actor's imagination.

Below is a list of simple items that you can find in almost any home. Have your players bring the items to your acting class, or gather them yourself. To run the improvisations, have two players take the stage, and then hand each of them one of the items. Tell the players that the props must play a significant role in the improvisation. Don't suggest a character relationship, a conflict, an obstacle, or any kind of setting. Just give them a signal to begin and let their imaginations take over.

As a fun alternative, tell them that they must use the prop as something other than what it actually is. This will force the actor to stretch his imagination even further. For example, a pencil might be used as a conductor's baton, a knitting needle, a dart, or anything else that its shape and size might suggest.

Use the following guide questions during your discussion of the improvisations:

1. Was the prop truly a central element of the improvisation?

2. Did the players make creative use of their props?

3. Would you have used the props differently?

1. aluminum foil

2. artificial flowers

3. ashtray

4. balloons

5. bar of soap

6. baseball cap

7. basket

8. belt

9. book

10. bookends

11. bud vase

12. buttons

13. candy dish

14. cassette tape

15. cellophane tape

16. cigar box

17. coasters

18. coffee can

19. coins

20. compact disc

21. costume jewelry

22. crayons

23. credit card

24. cup

25. drinking straws

26. driver's license

27. dustpan

28. earmuffs

29. earrings

30. envelope

31. eyeglasses

32. feather duster

33. felt marker

34. fork

35. frying pan

36. glass

37. glass jar

38. gloves

39. hairbrush

40. hand shovel

41. handkerchief

42. hat

43. key chain

44. keys

45. knitting needle

46. lamp shade

47. library card

48. light bulb

49. magazine

50. marbles

51. measuring cup

52. mixing bowl

53. nail file

54. napkins

55. newspaper

56. paper clip

57. paper cups

58. pen

59. pencil

60. pencil case

61. pepper shaker

62. picture frame

63. playing cards

64. postcards

65. purse

66. rags

67. ribbons

68. rubber ball

69. rubber band

70. ruler

71. salt shaker

72. saucer

73. scarf

74. shoehorn

75. shoelaces

76. shoes

77. soap dish

78. socks

79. sponge

80. spoon

81. stapler

82. steel wool pad

83. stick of chewing gum

84. stuffed animal

85. sunglasses

86. tape measure

87. tea bags

88. tea strainer

89. thermometer

90. ticket stub

91. tie

92. tie clip

93. tissues

94. toothbrush

95. toothpick

96. umbrella

97. wallet

98. wash cloth

99. wire hanger

100. wristwatch

8

Using Improvisations During Rehearsals

Many directors feel that they don't have time to use improvisations during rehearsals. They reserve it for their acting classes and use it only as a tool for training actors. Most directors typically begin their play rehearsals by holding a cast meeting, followed by a read-through of the entire play. Then comes a week or two of blocking rehearsals, followed by a few weeks of "I'll-stop-you-when-I-have-a-comment" rehearsals. Next comes a series of uninterrupted run-throughs, each one laboriously followed by the reading of the director's notes. Finally, technical and dress rehearsals take up most of the week before opening night. Throughout this entire process, improvisation is hardly used, if it is even used at all.

This is unfortunate because improvisation is one of the most valuable tools a director has at his or her disposal. It may be used during almost every stage of the rehearsal process, beginning before the actor even looks at a script. It can be used to help design the blocking and to help the actors become familiar with the play's settings. More important, it provides a way for the actor to investigate his character's past and understand his immediate and long-range objectives. Through the use of improvisation, the actor can explore his character's internal traits and find the best ways to externalize them.

While improvisation can effectively help the director accomplish some of his objectives, it should be noted that improvisation need not be used during every rehearsal, or even a majority of them. This chapter is intended only to offer a few alternatives to the traditional methods of reaching rehearsal goals. The director should use as many of them as will suit his particular rehearsal needs.

IMPROVING SCENE DESIGN

Tape the stage floor with masking tape to indicate where walls, doors, windows, arches, and stairs will be. Make sure that your measurements are completely accurate. Use combinations of chairs and boxes to suggest sofas, chairs, tables, and other furniture pieces. Fully explain to your cast exactly what everything represents.

Next, have your actors take the stage *without their scripts*. Tell them to imagine that they've walked into this place for the first time in their lives, and let them explore their surroundings. Next, conduct a few improvisations using the setting to initiate the action (see Chapter 6). As they move about the stage, ask yourself the following questions:

1. Do your actors move easily from one area of the stage to another, or do too many physical obstacles exist?

2. Are your actors naturally drawn to at least three areas of the stage?

3. In which areas of the stage do the actors seem to feel most comfortable?

4. Do the combinations of people sitting and standing at different areas of the stage look pleasing to the eye?

Use the information that you've learned to decide whether or not you will need to talk to your set designer about problems you've noticed.

PLANNING BLOCKING

Once you're satisfied with your set design, you can use improvisation to help design your blocking plan. One way to do this is to improvise situations similar to those in the play itself. This is best done before any scenes from the play have been rehearsed at all.

Before planning any blocking for a specific scene, have the actors who will be performing in that scene take the stage *without their scripts*. Even though it isn't necessary for your actors to have completely analyzed their characters' actions, objectives, justifications, and obstacles, they should at least be aware of their characters' dominant personality traits. Explain the basic situation and outcome of the scene to the actors, and then have them improvise the action. They shouldn't worry about specific lines or actions from the scene, but they should try to recreate the series of events that takes place in the scene as closely as possible. As the scene progresses, observe the movements and crosses that the actors make. Notice which areas of the stage they use. Note their physical relationships to each other.

Some of what you will learn by running these improvisations will be of little use to you as you plan your blocking. Some actors, especially inexperienced ones, will tend to make awkward crosses and form ineffective groupings. However, much of what you see will reveal some valuable clues for you to use as you create your overall blocking plan. To discover these clues, ask yourself the following questions after the scene has ended:

1. What motivated the actors to sit, stand, and make other movements and crosses?

2. Which acting areas and set pieces did the actors use most?

3. Throughout the course of the scene, how closely did the actors sit or stand beside each other? Why did they maintain those particular distances? Did the distances change at all throughout the scene?

4. When did the actors face each other or turn away from each other? What prompted them to do so?

5. How *much* movement took place throughout the scene?

6. Was there a great *variety* of movement?

7. How would you describe the pace or rhythm of the scene?

Use what you've learned to design your blocking, but be flexible. Listen to your actors when they tell you that they don't feel comfortable with a particular cross or movement, and don't be afraid to make last-minute changes. After listening to your actors' complaints, you may decide to stick with your blocking decisions. You as the director reserve the right to do so. However, it is in the best interest of the entire production that you explain your decisions to the actors involved and come to an understanding with them.

EXPLORING CHARACTER TRAITS

Before your actors have fully analyzed and developed their characters, you may wish to run a few improvisations for the purpose of exploring their characters' dominant personality traits. For example, if an actor who is in the initial stages of studying his character decides that one of his character's most dominant personality traits is his quick temper, you may run some improvisations using that character trait as an important element of the situation (see Chapter 2). This should be done before considering any of the character's specific actions and objectives from the play itself. In fact, the actor need not even play the role of his character during the improvisations. The purpose at this point should be to help the actor focus only on the moods, attitudes, and emotions of the character.

Here are some sample improvisations that a director of a production of Shakespeare's *Romeo and Juliet* might use.

Improvisations for Romeo

1. You've met a girl with whom you've instantly fallen in love. Share your feelings with her.

2. A friend of yours has been mortally wounded by someone you dislike. Promise your friend that you will seek revenge for what he did.

Improvisations for Juliet

1. Tell a trusted friend that you've decided to disobey your parents' wishes and secretly marry someone they hate.

2. Tell a friend that you'd rather die than live without your husband.

Improvisations for Mercutio

1. Tease a lovesick friend.

2. Respond to someone who's insulted your best friend.

Improvisation for Friar Laurence

1. Warn a friend not to be hasty about marrying a girl he just met and hardly knows.

Improvisation for the Nurse

1. Tell a friend that she's fallen in love with someone whose family is hated by your family.

Improvisation for Romeo, Mercutio, and Benvolio

1. Discuss the idea of crashing a party.

EXPLORING CHARACTER BACKGROUND

Usually it's important to understand what a character said and did prior to the action of the play in order to understand what the character says and does during the action of the play. One good way to study this prior action is to improvise the situations that took place before the play began. These situations may or may not involve other characters in the play. If they do, have those characters participate in the improvisation. If not, have other cast members play the needed roles.

Sometimes the action prior to the play isn't known. However, it still may be valuable to improvise situations that *could* have logically developed into the situations of the play. For example, if a character for some unknown reason shows a definite dislike toward another character in the play, it may be worthwhile to invent a scene that provides a reason ill feelings exist between the two. After improvising such a scene, the actors will have an experience they can use to explain their attitudes toward each other. Be careful, however, to make sure that the scene could have *logically* occurred. It will be counterproductive to create an experience that doesn't make complete sense to them.

The director of a production of *Romeo and Juliet* might wish to improvise the following situations:

1. Romeo on a date with Rosaline.

2. Rosaline breaking up with Romeo.

3. Romeo, Mercutio, and Benvolio doing something together.

EXPLORING OFF-STAGE ACTION

Playwrights have different reasons that some of the play's important action takes place off-stage. Some common reasons are:

1. The action is impossible to stage.

2. The playwright wishes to use only one setting and the scene involved takes place in another.

3. The playwright prefers not to show a violent or shocking act on-stage.

4. The off-stage action needs to come as a surprise to the audience.

Nevertheless, action that takes place off-stage can be just as important as the action that takes place on-stage. Improvising off-stage scenes immediately before rehearsing the scene that follows will help the actor become motivated to perform the character's on-stage actions. Let's say a scene from a play begins after a character has just had a vicious argument with someone moments before the scene opens. If that scene is faithfully recreated in an improvisational setting, the actor will more fully understand the feelings and thoughts that he is supposed to be experiencing on-stage.

The director of *Romeo and Juliet* might wish to improvise the following situations:

1. Capulet and Lady Capulet making a list of guests to invite to their feast.

2. Romeo hiding in Mantua.

3. Friar John quarantined in Verona.

4. Romeo on his way to the tomb.

5. Friar Laurence rushing to the tomb.

ACQUAINTING ACTORS WITH PROPS AND COSTUMES

Before your first dress rehearsal, have your actors improvise scenes using the costumes and props that they will be wearing and handling during the performance. This is especially important if the play is a period play, or if the props and costumes are particularly unusual.

Final Thought

Throughout this book, I have stressed the importance of improvisation as a tool for developing acting skills. Clearly, improvisation serves well to help the actor focus on his or her objectives, to react with spontaneity and honesty, to use the acting environment effectively, and to inspire imaginative and creative thinking. But improvisation is more than just a tool for helping the actor polish his technique. It is an art form in itself, which can and should be enjoyed and appreciated for its own entertainment value.

The idea of improvisation as an art form is nothing new. The performers of commedia dell'arte, a type of comedy popular in Italy during the sixteenth and seventeenth centuries, used no scripts but instead improvised upon a basic outline of a story. Improvisational theater has flourished ever since. One of the more famous examples is the Second City of Chicago, directed by Paul Sills.

It is my hope that this book will be valuable to actors and to students, teachers, and directors of theater. Happy improvising!